RENDEZVOUS WITH A RAINFOREST

By
Edie Bakker

Published by Shiloh House Books, 1340 Travis Lane,
Kaufman, TX 75142 USA

ISBN 978-1497547551

Cover design and internal sketches and maps by Janet Long
of Janet Long Designs

Cover photo of bird of paradise used by permission from Scotty
Graham
Photo of bird of paradise following chapter 26 used by permission
from Madang Visitors and Cultural Bureau, Papua New Guinea
All other photos by author or her family

So many people helped with this book that I cannot list them without someone feeling left out, however Linda Jones, Sue Mortimer, Sally Hoffman, Wayne Dye, Janet Long, my husband Rob Bakker and my writer's group Stone Soup come immediately to mind.

4

Table of Contents

Chapter 1 A Memory from Age Thirteen 9

Chapter 2 Rainforest Rendezvous 17

Chapter 3 Into the Rainforest 32

Chapter 4 The Cold Places 42

Chapter 5 Compromises and Exploitation.....................50

Chapter 6 Village in Conflict...62

Chapter 7 A Task Unfinished...70

Chapter 8 Mt. Hagen: "We Shouldn't Be Doing This…"77

Chapter 9 Memories..88

Chapter 10 Money or Friendships 94

Chapter 11 Which Way to the Mountain? 102

Chapter 12 A Terrifying Beast...115

Chapter 13 Black Tuesday..122

Chapter 14 Fishing 129

Chapter 15 The Carriers Sit..137

Chapter 16 A Thousand Foot Chasm 148

Chapter 17 On the Forehead of the Mountain 161

Chapter 18 Poison...169

Chapter 19 Rivers to Cross...172

Chapter 20 The Eye Leech..180

Chapter 21 Impossible Trail...188

Chapter 22 A Different Point of View 196

Chapter 23 Cultural Collision 202

Chapter 24 The Question of Tourism 206

Chapter 25 A Painful Goodbye 212

Chapter 26 Dance of the Birds of Paradise 216

R A I N F O R E S T..223

Appendix: THE MEMBERS OF THE EXPEDITION ..230

Lesser Bird of Paradise

THE RAINFOREST DOESN'T TALK

The rainforest doesn't talk.
It doesn't need to.
It whispers
with a thousand stirring leaves,
"I am at peace."
It pulses
with the steady flow of waterfalls, rivers and creeks,
"I am alive."
It cries
with the shrieks of cockatoos, parrots and eagles,
"I can feel pain."
It sparkles
with a million brilliant flowers,
"I am exuberant."
Its giant pillars draped in vines and bedecked with bromeliads touch
the sky and say,
"I am ancient."
A golden leaf slowly floating down inside its green cathedral,
whispers,
"... a holy place."
Its thousand harmonies of tropical song birds promise,
"I will enchant you."
But all of these whispers, pulses, cries and songs,
fall dead and silent,
In the terrible stillness after each tree
is ripped away from its roots.
Then there is only the wretched buzz of flies.

Chapter 1

A Memory from Age Thirteen

~~ Blissful birds of paradise
dance in the mysterious Hunstein
Mountain Rainforest, unaware of their
impending doom.

The deep black waters of Lake Wagu engulfed me in a sudden rush of relief from the tropical heat. I burst to the surface and treaded water looking at rainforest all around me. The splashes and laughs of my family almost covered the squawks of a pair of red and green eclectus parrots and a wild cockatoo flying by.

Around the edge of the lake, a thick dark green wall of trees and vegetation made the forest almost impossible to penetrate. Yet I had done so, several times a year since I was four years old. Once inside, past guarding swamps and myriads of spiders and bugs it was dark, cool and beautiful. As the two parrots that just flew overhead disappeared into the tops of the trees, I marveled at the mystery of that lush canopy where most birds and animals lived. It was a place I had never been and could never go. I could picture a tiny yellow leaf making its way down through the layers of the forest, past the red and yellow birds of paradise; past the multi-colored parrots; and past the furry tree kangaroo. I could see it lift ever so slightly as it swirled on down past the spotted cuscus with its wide eyes and the white and purple orchids and the baby trees, until finally landing softly on a pad of bright moist leaves in the dimness below. I viewed the forest as a teenage girl views a handsome young man she longs to be held by, but doesn't truly know. Would we ever connect?

A splash in the face from my sister diving in the water near me, snapped me out of my reverie. Warm surface water alternated with cooler water from the depths and I swam to a cool spot. A gray and white sea eagle soared and dived above us while herons flew silently toward their roosting tree. Pink and vermilion clouds in a blue sky appeared and then turned light gray as the day closed.

Daddy helped us into the boat so we could soap up. My family swam in the lake every evening. I dove in to rinse off. I felt grateful to be home from boarding school and back in Wagu Village among the Bahinemos of Papua New Guinea. I loved spending Christmas in this place. We often took advantage of the holidays to camp in the rainforest.

Mom and Dad had come here in early 1964 when we were babies and set up camp as missionaries among a tiny group of forest people.

Our boat sped to shore and we jumped out onto the rough shale beach filled with squishy snails, fish bones and small stones. It wasn't a place where one might lay in the sun.

A short walk huddled in wet towels brought us to our house. Always the first to don dry clothes, my mother immediately cooked dinner over our ancient kerosene stove, with ingredients from a kerosene fridge, under a kerosene lamp. Then Dad started the generator with a roar that covered the sound of the catfish frying, the villagers chattering and the frogs and crickets chirping. It lit up bright fluorescent lights which attracted swarms of tiny bugs through our screen walls.

Outside of the screen walls, village children laughed and swished long thin sticks in the air to catch bats. My brothers joined them while my sister and I helped with dinner and set the red formica table we had used since I was four years old. At that time we lived more primitively. We had no refrigerator so my mother cooked our food in a pressure cooker every day to preserve it. In those days the Bahinemo people were also much worse off. There were no children due to malaria, dysentery and other diseases. We ate wild game and fought off six inch jumping spiders, swarms of *roaches and mangy dogs that broke into our house through our bark floor. It was an inhospitable place for my three younger siblings and me.*

Things had improved. We now had a wood floor, and our screen walls fit tighter. We even had an indoor flush toilet.

Occasionally when Dad shut the generator off, we sat in the dark and listened to hundreds of frogs and watched the moon come up over the lake and the lightning in the clouds flicker above the surrounding rainforest.

We would enter that rainforest in a couple of days, but first there was to be a night of feasting and dancing, on this occasion, in celebration of the building of a new house.

Two days before the feast, I walked up the center of the village and visited the homes of my Bahinemo friends. They knew I loved animals and showed me a pet baby parrot and some captured giant fruit bats. A young cassowary wandered among the houses.

Some families had new babies, which I delighted in holding. But we were in many ways worlds apart. Their houses were dark and closed in, made of palm stem walls, smooth bark floors and palm leaf roofs. They were sparse with only open space for sleeping nets to be brought down from the rafters at night and a large clay fire place for each wife. Some men had one wife, some two. They said Fu nenei or "Come in" when I entered and Fui or "Go" when I left, but otherwise they didn't talk much. We didn't understand each other's ways of thinking. There were no kids my age to associate with or to learn more of the culture from.

In preparation for the feast, some of the women wove and dyed new grass skirts to wear at the dance, and a wild boar hung on a pole over a very hot fire. Along with other game, it would be divided throughout the village.

During the night, we children listened with curiosity and repulsion as a woman's loud groans floated through the rafters from another room in our house. Finally it arrived. A little cry rang out. Another healthy baby was born. "Quick, bring the scissors and string," my mother ordered a helper. Soon the baby's soft gurgle meant it had settled at the breast. Come daylight, my sister and I would be allowed to see it. Mom had saved many children.

On the next night, the night of the feast, Mom made a huge fire and stuffed a very large collection of empty cans with bread dough from a basin. She distributed the resulting small warm loaves to every family in the village.

My sister and I adjusted our colorful new grass skirts over our bathing suits. Daddy said we couldn't go topless this time, like the other women, so we tried to hide our bathing suits with long colorful leaves as much as possible. We wore all the bead and shell necklaces we owned and braided our hair. Then we finished the look with designs created from red paint made of annatto seeds, black charcoal and white clay.

We danced until dawn, at times resting with small children in our laps so their mothers could dance. Women found the sing-sing, or dance, easy. They simply walked in a swaying manner around a pole. The men, however, leaped and shouted around the outside of the ring. Lilting female voices echoed the men's leads in beautiful harmony. The songs mentioned rain, birds, the spirits of trees and people of old. I didn't really understand them, I was only told this. Bahinemo language still mystified me. After High School I would live and teach in Wagu village for a year and become much more fluent in Bahinemo. But in my early teens I communicated through Papua New Guinea's trade language, Tok Pisin, a simple language based on English.

In the morning the whole village spoke with hoarse voices from the singing. Everyone took naps and slept until afternoon.

We began packing to go into the rainforest. Various helpers assembled equipment, gathered food and mixed ingredients. Dad cleaned his shot gun. Mom baked cinnamon rolls and measured oatmeal and rice. We kids were mostly at a loss and in the way. We had nothing to pack except two cotton dresses, or shorts for the boys, and our bathing suits. The mood was tense and hectic and there was a lot of frustration for the whole family. Quiet orderly people didn't attempt trips like this. I couldn't wait until the next day.

In the morning we loaded our boat and Dad haggled with the villagers over who would be our guides. Finally we settled on two young men, Yashio and Wamseli, and pushed off from shore. As soon as the engine revved up a cool breeze blasted our faces. The lake was wide and calm, reflecting the sky and the dark green hills. How I loved its refreshing beauty.

We traveled about fifteen minutes and came to a shallow area indicated by scattered blue lilies and pads. We begged to stop and eat the stems and the seeds, and Dad managed to slow the boat alongside a few of the lilies, which we pulled up. We didn't worry about picking too many. They would be here forever. The seeds tasted like soft nuts. I savored most, the crunchy, juicy, delicious lily stems. Some of the stems were ten feet long and we had to peel every inch a little at a time to avoid lake germs. What a delicacy!

Dad let me stand at the bow and guide him through the lilies to the only spot on the shore where we could enter the rainforest. Where the tall sharp kunai grass barrier thinned out a little, we plowed through and landed ashore. Hundreds of spiders and grasshoppers leaped into the boat and we all squealed and dodged them, exiting quickly. We gathered our loads and Yashio and Wamseli cut us strong walking sticks.

We stepped under the trees immediately, but to get to the ridge we had to traverse a swamp of sago palms. The fetid red mud in the swamp was waist deep and made of rotten plants. It stank. Six inch thorns grew on every branch and floated in the ooze. We walked on sticks buried in the mud and used our walking sticks liberally. Both happy and miserable at the same time, we listened to the flocks of lorikeets above us, the screeches of parrots and the wonderful varying songs of the Mynah bird. Butterflies fluttered everywhere.

After half an hour we stepped into a clear running stream with rocks on the bottom. We stumbled gingerly over the rocks and enjoyed the cool fresh water. Before we ascended the ridge we took off our muddy shoes and socks and rinsed our legs and feet. We put the footwear in our packs. We wouldn't need it until the way back.

Peace and quiet accompanied us while climbing the ridge. The canopy far above kept us in shade and the trees stood far enough apart to allow us to see for some distance. Every hour we stopped and Mom distributed crackers and cheese or the cinnamon rolls. We each carried our own canteens and drank frequently. Bird calls continued to entertain us.

Finally, at the top of the ridge, we sat on the soft dirt and rested. After resting, we turned our efforts to going down the other side of the ridge, where huge beautiful trees clung to the steep slope. Our knees soon ached from the arduous climb down. Wamseli cut some of the bark from a cinnamon tree so we could chew it on the way.

At last we came to a creek covered with hundreds of kinds of bushes. It flowed down over bright shiny rocks. Any chance to walk down a fallen tree made the trail easier and more interesting. In places the bright orange flowers of the liana vine littered the ground around us.

The creek at last joined the river, creating high banks and sandbars. A small island stood in the middle of the river. We called this place Bani. The Hunstein River swirled softly around logs, bends and curves with crystal clear water. You could see to the bottom of its five or six feet deep water holes.

We made our camp on the high bank. With the help of Wamseli and Yashio, we made a shelter using saplings tied with vines, a bark floor and a tarpaulin roof. We had to be up off of the moldy, bug-ridden ground. The guides built a fire-place up off of the ground too, at counter level, for easy tending. They did this by packing clay into a sapling platform.

When we finished our chores, us kids headed straight for the cool refreshing river. We played with the current, floating with it, fighting it and trying to swim across it. We kept our eyes open in the clear water and dove for beautiful rocks on the river bottom. Our favorites were white crystals that reflected light and seemed to glow. Dad sometimes threw them in the current so we could race to see who could collect the most.

At night as I lay on my mat, I listened to a chorus of sounds. Owls and nightjars, as well as bugs that beeped, clicked and buzzed entertained the ears. Mom and Dad slipped away to be alone in the river. I could hear them laughing. I also heard the growl of a crocodile. I was scared for my parents, but they came back. There were things that glowed here and there outside my net; lichens, scorpions, moldy leaves. Things rustled in the bushes.

The sun woke up multitudes of exotic birds. Hornbills arrived and lured us out of our nets. These enormous birds sounded like jet planes when they flew. It seemed like they were coming from a mile away. They landed in trees nearby to watch us. In turn, we watched them as they made laughing sounds while cavorting from branch to branch. Their three foot black and white bodies, white or gold heads and large carved beaks made quite a spectacle. After breakfast and a cold morning swim, I lay on a warm sandbar and looked up at the trees where white cockatoos swooped up and down hundreds of feet, dancing in the air to impress their mates.

While on the sandbar I surveyed all sorts of crystal and mineral rocks. Elegant pieces of driftwood and various fruits were washed onto the shore. They came in all kinds of shapes, sizes and colors. Flowers filled the trees and bushes.

In honor of Christmas, the men brought home a two and a half foot tall Victoria Crowned Pigeon. They were poaching but nobody cared about this rainforest, and anyway there were hundreds of the birds. I gazed at this one's beautiful blue and purple feathers and white laced crown, now useless on its lifeless body and asked if I could have it. "Of course," my father replied and cut it off. Something in me felt barbaric about this, but I didn't yet know what it was. I laid the crown in the sun to dry and someone plucked the rest of the bird.

Mom dressed it and cooked it on a spit over the fire. We pretended it was turkey but more tender and delicious. Mom made a cake over the fire too, and we each picked flowers and fruits to give to each other in a symbolic gift exchange.

Dad cut a large vine near a deep pool in the river and we swung and splashed for the rest of the afternoon.

The next day, my brother and I were lying on the sandbar gazing up at the trees.

"Mom says the world is going to end in a terrible tribulation and no one will escape persecution," I said off handedly.

"Yeah, but it will never reach here," he said.

"I guess you're right," I said. "No one would ever find us here. This is the safest most remote place in the world."

"How about we build a house in that tree over there," he said. "They'll never find us in the trees."

"I get that one over there with the spread out branches."

We lay silently in the sand contemplating the future. How I wish I could stay here forever, I thought. No one could ruin this.

Tom, Edie, Jamey, and Joy at Bani

Edie as a child in the rainforest

Blythe's Hornbill

2 1/2 foot tall Victoria Crowned Pigeon

Chapter 2

Rainforest Rendezvous

~~ *"Woa woa woa," rose the loud call of a bird-of-paradise. A stick fell from above and landed with a tiny swish in the silence. I could feel the soft moss surrounding my toes. Everything was cold and damp. Mist shrouded the trees - the giant magnificent trees of Mount Hunstein. They stood proud, never encountered before our visit. We tiptoed back to nurse our tired bodies at camp leaving the holy place alone. I would leave the rain forest for the U.S. to start a whole new life on my own. The trees would stay.~~*

Fifteen years later I am married and live in the U.S. with my husband and two kids. I struggle to sit up in my bed, fighting the disorientation and the scenes clinging to my brain. I see bulldozers and hear the crash of timber as magnificent giant trees crumble to the ground. I see huge roots caked with dirt wrenched from the ground, and smell crushed vegetation. I awake drenched with sweat. The vision turns into thoughts and I shudder. I know these trees. They are the trees of my heart from the virgin rainforest where I was raised. The scenery in my head doesn't match the Dallas house around me, so I realize it's a nightmare.

Yet nothing feels more real than the vision that engulfs me. Houses and gray buildings replace the trees. A familiar creek where my brothers and sister and I learned to swim dries up. At one point canoes on Wagu Lake are required to stop at stoplights. The overwhelmed villagers do not know how to cope.

A canoe stoplight… This is too much. It really is another nightmare, not prophesy. I have had this nightmare twice before. Everything on the other side of the world must still be the same as ever. I would have heard something. How I long for news from

Papua New Guinea; from the village of Wagu, from the Hunstein Rainforest where I grew up.

But, what if the nightmares are prophetic?

I struggle to get the kids off to school. I clean the counters but leave the rest of the house. Scenes of my childhood flash before me for the rest of the day,

--Eating the sweet wild fruit we called "sinabi."

--Following a creek through the rainforest with my family, and floating the cool clear current back down to our dugout canoe.

--Swinging on vines over a river from huge trees and dropping into a deep pool.

--Climbing and drinking the water of the waterfalls at age seven.

--The day Wamseli carved my boyfriend's name on a tree on Mount Hunstein.

At one time Wagu, the village we lived in, consisted of a group of hunters and gatherers drawn out of the Hunstein mountain forests by colonial style "kiaps", or government officers, to the edge of a hostile disease ridden swamp. There the people, who called themselves Bahinemos, could be reached by river to combat their cannibalism. When my parents came there as missionary/linguists with life saving medicine, no babies had survived infancy for eight years. My Dad became an anthropologist out of fascination for the ways of this tiny tribe. Now, twenty-five years later, is the Wagu lifestyle about to change drastically again?

In the afternoon, Mom and Dad who, by now also live in Dallas, drop by. Dad gives me a hug and some books and we chat idly for a while about news from my other grown siblings scattered around the U.S. "Oh, by the way," he says casually, on his way out the door. "Did you hear they are going to log the Hunstein Range?"

The world swirls and I must clutch the wall. I am stunned. It can't be. I tell him about my dreams. He looks disturbed, but shrugs. "There's not much we can do about it," he says. "The forest has already been offered to the big companies in Japan."

I can't hear anymore. Somehow I show him out.

It is two in the morning and I haven't slept. Scenes from the nightmares rush through my mind. Over and over the bulldozers push back the trees. Soon nothing but dirt and grass remain. The call of the bird-of-paradise is silent.

Finally I can stand it no longer. I get up and write, without stopping, without hesitating and without correcting. I pour out my heart. I send the letter to the president of the National Geographic Society explaining the beauty, the isolation and the uniqueness of the Hunstein Rainforest along with the history of its 500 men, women and children.

I seal my precious letter and drop it in the mail box at the door. It seems so vulnerable. Soon the mail man takes it away and I do not hear anything.

It was never a consideration that I would be able to stay in Papua New Guinea which was the only environment I knew growing up. Missionary children went to college; period. Ten years have passed since I left Papua New Guinea, the beloved forest and its people. It's 1988 and I have been unable to escape the U. S. since; trying to fit in jobs, marriage, kids and strained finances. I've left my childhood home behind, but it remains always a deep wound in my heart. I cannot get over the pain of losing my home country.

Finally, after a year, a letter arrives from the society.

"We are so sorry but we do not involve ourselves in political matters of this sort," it says. I read the short letter over and over. Crushed, I set it aside.

About six months later I get a call. It's from a professor at Yale University. In shock, I lock myself in the bathroom so the kids won't disturb me. We talk about the forest for half an hour. We talk about the rare birds, the animals and the trees.

This phone call is followed by another, this time from Harvard. Then, I get a letter from the Papua New Guinea government thanking me for bringing the situation to their attention, though not promising to do anything. Somehow word of my letter is spreading.

Finally Dr. Sy Sohmer, from the Bishop Museum of Hawaii contacts me. "We are going to do something about this," he reassures me after we talk for an hour.

Later he calls me back. He has spoken with his friends at the National Geographic. They are going to sponsor an expedition. I am invited to go along. There is the possibility that I could write an article. The rest is a blur. But I remember rolling across the floor over and over with my dog and yelling "YES! YES! YES! I'M GOING HOME!"

Soon I receive tickets in the mail to go to the magazine's headquarters in Washington D.C. for an interview. It is more than I can comprehend. My Dad says I won't get the job. I have no degrees, no formal experience in writing and I am only 28 years old. He is trying to protect me from disappointment.

Skirts and blouses lay across my bed along with suit jackets, necklaces and a couple of sweaters. Sweaters in the summer! Friends tell me this is the style, but it doesn't make sense. I don't understand anything that my friend JoAnne from church says about style except that it seems a jacket might be useful for the weather in D.C. Of course the jacket she picks is the stylish kind, not the warm kind

Then there are the shoes. High heels!

My feet formed walking barefoot or in flip flops. My toes spread apart. I can't balance on high heels. How will I walk in them? We settle on some moderate heights. The suede pumps are for day and the shiny ones for evening. I shrug my shoulders in resignation and sigh.

JoAnne, who always seems to be "in," moves on to a different horror. I will have to wear makeup. My lips are a natural red, my skin smooth and tan. I don't own any makeup. Fortunately she chooses the colors for me after selecting five outfits and testing my skin. She shows me twice what to buy and how to put it on.

On the curb at 5:00 am waiting for a taxi a week later, all dressed up in pumps and lipstick, I feel glamorous, dignified and glad for JoAnne's help.

The elegance of the hotel and the luxury of roast chicken breast stuffed with brie and raspberries provide me with a glimpse of what is to come. The next morning, while I wait nervously for my interview, I watch National Geographic's slide show in their lobby. Tears come to my eyes and I feel like I belong in their multicultural exploratory world. I have looked at the pictures of every *National Geographic* I could get my hands on since I was seven, so many of the pictures are familiar to me.

The interview takes place over a lavish meal in a private room. All the heads of the magazine are there; dignified older gentlemen in tailored suits. I am more grateful than ever for the makeover. The butler fills my glass with champagne and so begins a protocol which I am unfamiliar with. Some kind person whispers hints to me. I am to take the first bite of each course. I must calculate every word I say with utmost care. The food is exotic and the pressure intense, but somehow I am relaxed. This is so far out of my league; so fantastic, that I feel I have nothing to lose. I am in it for the ride.

The completion of the main course brings on the verbal grilling. What would I have to say if I wrote the article? What is my theme or my goal? They look at the pictures I brought and an unpublished religious manuscript I wrote on culture. It is the only thing I have ever written. We talk about a project I did in high school studying egrets on Wagu Lake. I tell them about the forest and the threat to the trees. They eye me intently with every response, taking in every nuance and poking at any inconsistency.

I am aware that I must reach deep into memories I have closed myself off from. I have always missed the rainforest so much that it hurts to remember what is no longer mine. But now those memories may bring about the only chance I have to save the place that was and still is so precious to me.

The officials seem more interested in the village of Wagu than they are in preserving the rainforest. The hardest questions are about religion. "Yes, I am a Christian," I reply, "and so are the Bahinemo people who own the forest. They became Christians because they were terrified of evil spirits and Christianity offered a way to escape them." This seems to satisfy them, much to my relief. I don't want my personal religion to get in the way of the monumental goal that lies before me. I believe bringing the story of the Hunstein Rainforest to the world through *National Geographic* might save it.

I get the job.

My husband, Rob, and our two children will join the expedition with me in exchange for a cut in my pay. The National Geographic Society sponsors the expedition which is put on by the Bishop Museum of Hawaii in conjunction with the Wau Ecology Institute of Papua New Guinea. Every one of us involved desires a close look at the virgin rainforest, much of which has never before been explored, even by the Bahinemos. I am interested in the future of Bahinemo society. The magazine and I are determined to bring the forest to the attention of governments, environmental agencies and the general population. The battle to save the Hunstein Rainforest has begun. I am really on my way. My grand rendezvous with the rainforest begins.

National Geographic wants me to take along whatever my husband and I think will make our family comfortable for the three and a half month journey. We can buy whatever we need. I am eager to show off my children to the Bahinemos. Gabriel, at age eight and Sarah, age five, long to see the other side of the world. My husband will be my body guard in a country where travel can be dangerous. We select tents, backpacks and lots and lots of little camping gadgets I haven't even heard of. Of all of these, the plain metal cooking rack and a simple fold up stool seem the most valuable, along with the water filter. What fun.

Just before we leave, Sarah playfully takes a pair of scissors to her hair. To fix it, it has to be cut so short that she looks like a boy. At first I am furious with my poor child, but how can she know she is about to be in a magazine that will go out all over the world? I get her ears pierced and this identifies her as a girl again.

I am in a daze the whole way to Port Moresby, the capital city of Papua New Guinea or "PNG." I simply can't believe I am truly back. We are ushered into the high security gates of the mission hostel where we spend the night. We have chosen to stay in mission stations to cut expenses and for a better environment for our children.

When I smell the smoke of the cooking fires and hear the PNG music coming from the neighbors' radios; when I listen to the laughter of children chattering in the local language – I know this is my country and come out of my daze with elation.

After spending the night in Port Moresby, we move to the northern coastal town of Wewak. At 6:00 am I wake up and go outside to sit on a hill overlooking the ocean outside our apartment. Old familiar bird cries come from a nearby patch of forest. The slow rhythm of the soft waves rolls in from the Pacific Ocean. My love for this country is almost unbearable. It feels as though I am about to reunite with a long lost lover.

Rob and I take a trip into town with the children. We wear bathing suits and bring snorkels and some borrowed inner tubes. The missionaries warn us it's too dangerous to go swimming.

"Why?" we ask.

"Because the town's people will steal everything in your car," they reply.

"Why don't you lock the car?" we say. They haven't thought of that.

The reef in the bay in town is wonderful. Brightly colored little fish scurry through and around shimmering live coral. We have a fabulous time - all except little Sarah who thinks the whole thing about swimming with fish is a terrible idea. Gabriel, though, is mesmerized.

While we are in Wewak we meet our photographer, Jay Dickman, a handsome man with angular features and a quiet no-nonsense attitude. I will be working closely with him throughout the trip. We also meet the American scientists from Hawaii; including Dr. Sohmer who suggested *National Geographic* hire me to write the article. Dr. Sohmer is kind and very personable. His eyes sparkle and his handshake is warm. Dr. Allison is famous for his work in the area. He is tall, with a serious expression and demeanor.

We invite the scientists to our temporary home for dinner. At the market I buy squash greens. Papua New Guineans eat the soft green tips of the squash vine as well as the squashes themselves. The squash greens are a little hairy but delicious with butter. I serve these to the scientists and the photographer along with fresh steak and potatoes. While the men are gracious, they seem as if they would have preferred to have eaten at their hotel. Perhaps it is the greens. The whole visit is awkward and conversation is scarce.

As I lie in bed that night, I think about this third world nation. In 1975, with only one paved road, one stop light and one very impressive parliament building, Papua New Guinea established a governing system that functions smoothly to this day. It has never had a war and never experienced serious inflation. So far, it has managed to stand against the tides of economic repression and terrorism that have buffeted so many of the world's young developing countries. Will multi-national companies ruin this island world?

The next morning our family and photographer, Jay Dickman, fill the little Cessna 185 airplane to capacity. Jay will follow me from here on with few exceptions. The pilot is David Rowe, whose parents I had known as a child. He remembers me and allows me to fly the plane over an area of thick kunai grass. Mountains loom on the horizon so he grabs the yoke again.

Soon we circle gracefully over the Sepik River, a swirling quarter mile of muddy water which looks as if it's boiling, and alight gently on the grassy air-strip of Ambunti. My missionary/anthropologist father, Dr. Wayne Dye, has come to meet us in an old red flat bed truck which I recognize. He gathers up my children in his arms, just as he did his own kids so many times years before. My parents have coincidentally chosen to return to the village at this time after being away. They will be a tremendous help to us. Familiar sights and sounds overwhelm me. I find no evidence of the pending environmental storm.

We stay in the Pacific Island Ministries mission hostel at Ambunti. Once a government station, Ambunti has grown to a small, somewhat dilapidated town divided into two sides. On the north side is a tiny store, a small commercial lodge and the mission hostel. On the other side of the airstrip is a hill with a Catholic mission, an ornately carved court pavilion, and a small "hospital" compound which Americans might consider a mere clinic. Deeply rutted dirt track roads connect a hodge-podge of tin and thatch roofed houses draped in light green foliage.

I watch Gabriel and Sarah play the same games on the same steps as I did so long ago. My memories are coming back. It is almost as though I never left. Soon we will be meeting the

Bahinemo people of Wagu. My husband and I will be reunited with
them at last. As a teenager Rob met the Bahinemos and made
several friends when he took his holidays with my family in Wagu. I
wonder how they will respond to us after we've been gone for so
long.

I gaze across the swirling Sepik River. It is now evening.
Rose colored clouds drape enticingly over the Hunstein hills twenty
miles away in a gorgeous sunset. Clouds are pink, not red with smog
like the sunsets in the U.S. I am back in my world. Tears of
anticipation, joy and nostalgia come to my eyes. Then I notice Jay
circling discretely in the back ground watching for opportunities to
photograph me. I go back into the hostel.

At night we are each given mosquito nets that hang from the
ceiling. Screen walls take the place of air conditioners. The roaring
generator for the town doesn't go off until 9:00 pm. When it does, it
is replaced by loud frogs, screaming and flapping fruit bats, night
birds and unfamiliar human noises, not to mention the steady hum of
mosquitoes. It is a good thing Rob and I are in the same room as the
children. We are tired and sleep well in spite of all the noise.

The day dawns overcast, so we wait until afternoon to set
out. It requires both my father's aluminum boat and a dugout canoe
to carry all of us including several expedition members and supplies.
We plan to go up the Sepik River and then up the Hunstein Channel
to the village.

In spite of our geographic position in the tropics, cold damp
air clings to our lightly clad bodies. We buzz along over
unfathomable amounts of brown water heading past the vast swamp
which makes up most of the East Sepik Province. After a mile or
two, we turn and head across turbulent boils toward a barely
decipherable gap in the ten foot high grass which lines the bank.
Seconds before we reach our channel, we run into tea colored "black
water", indicative of rich forests at its source.

We follow the twisting channel toward dark green hills.
Occasional sparse trees punctuate the grass lining both sides of the
channel. These trees are often crowded with herons, cormorants and
various hawks. As we zoom by, bright red and green eclectus parrots
scream and race away from us. Little white egrets, pied herons and

many smaller birds scatter at our approach. Once, rounding a bend, we come across the turbulent wake of a crocodile.

For an hour and a half we follow the channel's twists and turns. Those of us in the long, narrow, dugout canoe must be careful to keep our balance. The dark water reflects a perfect image of the scenery. Finally we cut right into the hills themselves and wait breathlessly for the peaceful appearance of Wagu Lake. In an unexpected moment, the channel opens and there it is. The lake is a couple of miles across and shimmers with the reflection of a silver sky on millions of tiny waves. The Hunstein Range rises a misty blue behind the distant dark green shore, like a painted panorama.

But the photographer is getting anxious. In fact, he is very anxious.

"Turn back!" He shouts to the drivers, and the entourage slows. "The light isn't right. I can't take pictures!" We are all shocked. It is drizzling and passengers, filled with the hope of a dry comfortable house, grumble and complain. It is incomprehensible to turn back, but turn back we do, retracing twenty miles of winding river to arrive back at Ambunti just before dark. At dusk the tired and confused men unload everything. We each get the same guest beds again. Through this event we are all made aware of how things must be handled for the magazine. The photographer will be boss.

We are up in the morning as soon as the sun's pink rays shine across the Sepik River. Everything is reloaded the same way as the day before. We zigzag up the channel again, the boats loaded to maximum capacity. Sarah's eyes are wide with wonder at the birds. Gabriel sits with Rob so I can't see his eyes, but he is always amazed at new things. Our children are very curious about the world and this trip is amazing to them.

This time, in a sudden moment, the lake lies smooth like a mirror before us. The Hunstein Range looms above it in a misty haze. A tiny brown speck amid shades of green on the opposite shore is Wagu village. In the air hangs the sweet pungent smell of lilies. The sunshine is perfect.

The shore is covered with rough pebbles, fish bones, grasshoppers and flies. It immediately swarms with precious, beloved people. Villagers crowd in from all directions hugging us, clinging to us, smiling and laughing and lifting my children. We catch each other's eyes. I can see and feel thousands of silent words, and moving tears, in the midst of astonishment.

My mother, Sally, welcomes us to my old village home. She has a gracious gift of hospitality and can cook a gourmet meal with few ingredients. She will make the children's stay in the village more than comfortable. The children run in the house to see Grandma.

Nothing about the physical structure of the village has changed since I lived here eleven years ago. I find this uncanny. I have travelled and moved around so much since I left that it seems unnatural to touch the same palm stem walls, look out on the same mango trees and hibiscus bushes, walk the same mud paths, and even get a drink from that old kerosene refrigerator. No development has taken place except for an expansive school on a nearby peninsula.

The people, however, have changed. They have grown old. Thirty five is the average life expectancy, and girls marry soon after puberty. This is just like the experience of the fictional children of Narnia when they stepped back into the wardrobe after a year and found everyone had grown up. While I have grown to young middle age, the people in my peer group are now grandparents. At seventeen I spent a year starting the first village school. Now as I look around me the young boys from my school have beards, worn faces and serious eyes. Those little playful girls now carry their own children in their arms. My relationships with individuals have melted in a sea of time. The little boy named Yeital whom I remember putting grasshoppers on the chairs of the girls in my school, is now a quiet father. I no longer know these people.

A curious crowd of children surround Gabriel and Sarah from the minute we arrive at my parents' house. Sarah's blond hair and blue eyes are a sharp contrast to the dark skinned, curly haired village children. Gabriel, who has brown eyes and brown hair, stands out never-the-less with his light skin and strange language. Uncertain how to respond to the crowd, he entertains them with antics which make them roar with laughter.

Most of the people in the village have taken on new Western names. Now, with their names and faces both changed, I must learn to recognize individuals by their personalities alone. This is a slow process yet I soon sink back into the Bahinemo world and spend most of my time outside, listening and observing. One person, easy to recognize by his doe eyes, wide head and habit of stuttering was my star pupil when I was a teen. He has taken the Western name of Jim. He is married to Bahio, a sweet girl from a neighboring tribe. The two of them work for my parents and they quickly form a special bond with my children. Jim and Bahio take the kids on walks around the village and Bahio carries Sarah everywhere. Sarah especially enjoys this, and it becomes obvious I should hire them as official babysitters while we travel through the forest.

I have so many interviews to conduct. I must learn to understand the politics and culture of the village. I interview San Bawi, for instance, a Bahinemo woman raised in Wagu. "San" is the proper Bahinemo address for a woman. "Ma" is the form for a man. These titles are for formal use or to show respect.

"How many children do you have, San Bawi?" I ask.

She looks puzzled, and then begins to count: "Robert, Michael, plus the two girls, that makes four, and then Lona and Dona. Oh yeah and --Wida. He's at school. Is that 6? No…wait a minute… 1,2,3,4...7! I guess." She beams. "I have seven children!" She is proud and happy about the fact.

Why has this brilliant woman never stopped to count her children before? She lives in a world not governed by numbers, not bound by schedules; a world where there are some things which are constant - the sun, the seasons, the incessant spread of vegetation. There are other things that occur unpredictably: children, wild game, thunderstorms, malaria, death and love. People do not plan, cause or control either type. But coming events will force them to plan, cause and take control of their future.

The Bahinemo people are and always have been hunters and gatherers. Historically, they are the small remnant of several tribes who speak different languages. Dwindled down by intertribal war and disease, small family groups alone in the rainforest made treaties with each other for mutual protection and to obtain wives.

At some point they agreed to speak one language, "Bahinemo", meaning "our talk", and gathered to form a community.

In the 1950's civilization and the Australian government drew them out of the forest to the river system and the lake, where they were no longer protected from epidemics. The swamps near the lake exposed them to more malaria mosquitoes, and their numbers dwindled even faster. That is why no babies survived for at least eight years. This changed when my parents arrived in 1964 and brought Western medicine to the Bahinemos. From that point on, their population grew, and in 1968 they built the permanent village of Wagu, adopting the sturdy houses of the river people.

From my interviews it seems that so far modern changes have been primarily positive. However, due to cultural traditions, customs, tastes, knowledge, habits and history, it is obvious that the Bahinemos depend entirely on the Hunstein rainforest. Logging the forest will have a drastic effect on the villagers of Wagu. I know I must go into the forest again.

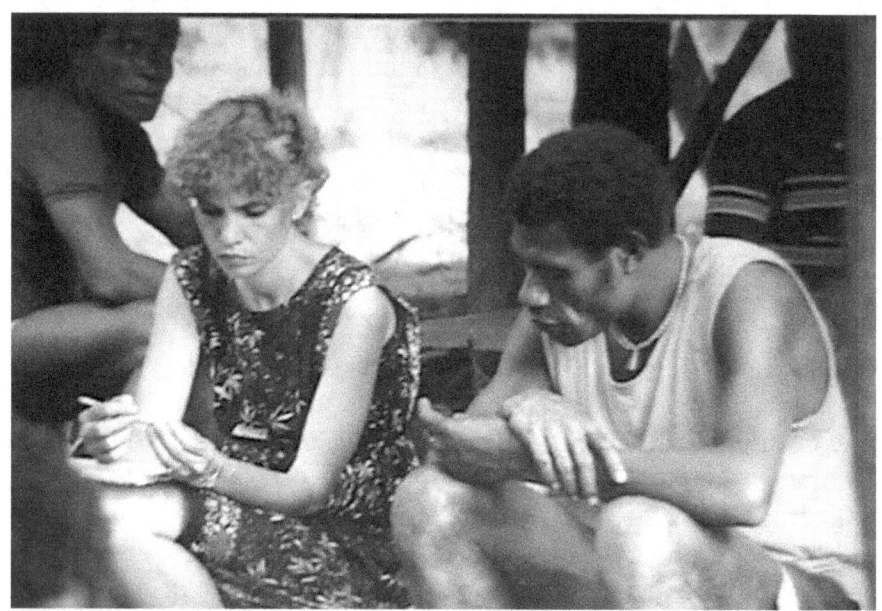

Edie conducting interviews for NGS

Traditional Bahinemo house

Chapter 3

Into the Rainforest

*~~ "Chump, chump, chump" went the stone
axes, echoing in the hollow they created. Aromatic
chunks of cedar flew in every direction. I picked up a
nearby piece of the soft, pink wood and held it to my
face to breathe in the fresh smell. Then my tall, dark
skinned friend, Bayei handed me a small, round,
green colored fruit. I bit into the rich flavor and we
both laughed as we tried to rub off the wax it left on
our teeth. Maybe I should take some of this fruit back
to camp for Mommy, I thought, --but my grass skirt
had no pockets. I tried to climb up a giant stump left
by a fallen tree, cut by the grownups to carve a
canoe. It was too high for a four year old like me.
Bayei lifted me up and I could see trees all around.
The sweet smelling stump was like a tower. Soon it
was time to go, so Bayei hoisted my bundle of
firewood tied together with vines onto my bare back
and I followed her footsteps into the forest. ~~*

We commence the expedition part of our journey on the
fourth day in Wagu village. We invade the trail into the rainforest in
the morning with a long entourage. The scientists began their trek
into the Hunstein rainforest ahead of us. Their large assembly is
progressing rapidly.

The plants and animals in Papua New Guinea are quite
different from all others in the world except Australia, with whom a
few species are shared. The island includes both Papua of Indonesia
on the west and Papua New Guinea on the east. A towering
mountain range travels its length. Mount Hunstein rises 5,000 feet
out of the Sepik river basin in the north. A vast, almost sea level
swamp completely isolates it from other highlands. Through eons of
this isolation, special plants and some small animals have evolved

that are different from those of the rest of New Guinea. In order to study the different levels of the 600 square mile Hunstein Forest, our scientists gradually attempt to work their way up the mountain.

More times than I can remember, my family has hiked into Bani, the first camp of the expedition.

On our way we must cross a swamp where women are processing sago. Sago is the primary starch eaten in the lower lands of Papua New Guinea.

The men have split open the trunk of a sago palm and the woman are pounding its pithy center into shreds using stone tools and modern tools made to imitate them. The stone pounders work better than the modern ones, I am told.

When they gather a mound of pith, they wash it through an ingenious set of sieves made from various plant fibers. The sieves are set along the inside of a trough made of the wide stem of a palm leaf. They dip water from a nearby stream and mix it with the pith. Then they drain it so the starch filters down through the system and settles into a bark catching bowl. Next the women pour off the excess liquid and wrap the starch in porous bark which they carry in a string bag. As they walk home it drains further down their backs until it becomes a fine powder. The string for the bag is made of fibrous tree bark. All in all I count thirteen different forest plants which the villagers use for gathering and preparing sago.

Jim and Bahio carry the children through the nasty, muddy swamp. Once we are past it, we all wash our shoes in a clear creek at the foot of a ridge.

Birds call out in the stillness, creating music unlike anything man could ever make. Here and there a stream trickles in the background. I choose to walk bare foot as I did growing up so I can flick off any leeches with ease before they have a chance to stick into my skin. I dig my toes into the soft, bare earth to climb the ridge.

Two hours after leaving Wagu, my family, Jay, the babysitters and twenty-five of the Bahinemo villagers hired on as carriers and accompanying us as friends descend into the Hunstein River Valley. The path down the ridge is steep, and we need walking sticks to keep from straining our knees. On the way we stop and show Jay the cinnamon bark tree.

Leaves, fruit and flowers litter the ground as we reach the valley. The forest is open, sheltered by the dense canopy of leaves above, creating a dusk which prevents smaller plants from growing. Lorikeets and lories, similar to parakeets and parrots but more colorful, screech over us in flocks seeking nectar and fruit. Almost all the plants in a rainforest bear flowers and fruit in their time.

For the first time in eleven years I feel at home. I trust the unvarying temperature that partly defines tropical forests. I am safe because I know what is around me. I feel comfortable. I exult in the beauty, the complexity, the predictability and the awesome power of the living system that surrounds me.

As we walk along I decide to interview San Moyali about what the trees mean to her.

"Trees are our only source of income," San Moyali says. San Moyali is a tall, mature woman with wisdom and poise and a natural red tint to her hair. She has always been my mom's best friend in the village. It seems to me saving the trees can only happen if the income from them is replaced.

First Moyali tells me "A man can get $100 to $200 for a tree that has been hollowed out enough to float down river where it will become a canoe."

"How else can you make money?" I ask. "Is there any other way to work?"

"No. There are never any jobs around here. We can gain some money by selling sago. If we can get it to the market in time we might get a dollar or two but it takes all day to gather one bag, and it spoils quickly."

"Another thing we can sell is grubs. If they're smoked and wrapped, they're worth 10 cents. We also sell turtles and smoked wild pig, but they don't bring much. A woven and painted string bag made from tree bark could provide $2 if it's large. It takes many days of work to make one. We can sell jungle fruits and herbs sometimes. Lots of kinds exist. Of course a crocodile skin is worth $6 after a couple of years of raising it in a pond."

Clearly no other known sources of income compare with cutting trees. I am distressed. There have got to be other ways.

After the discussion of income, I realize everything Moyali needs and owns comes from the forest. Tools made of wood, stone and vines; skirts made of palm fibers; bags of bark string; bowls made of palm sheaths; bows and arrows made of bamboo, vines and wood; canoes carved out of trees; houses made of bark, wooden poles, vines and palm leaves and stems; all require the forest in order to exist. Wild game and fish are still the primary source of protein. Wild herbs and fruits are the main source of vegetable nutrition, and sago is still preferred as a regular staple over expensive commercial rice. Almost their entire inventory of material goods depends on the forest. What would they do without them? I wonder. How would they live without their rainforest?

Like so many of the complex things in life, those who are not familiar enough to understand the rainforest often presume it to be harsh and unpredictable. In fact, its greatest beauty lies precisely in that it is so predictable. Those fortunate enough to know it well have their eyes open to the most advanced and intricately developed system on earth. They see a storehouse of living treasures, each involved and dependent on the routines and cycles of the other. They feel the very pulse of creation. This is the most important gift the rainforest has to offer. These millions of treasures all functioning together are intrinsically valuable like a coral reef or the universe. Losing this forest would be unthinkable.

We follow nature's fallen logs down the ravine which is the start of Bani creek. The creek bed is made up of shiny, flat, mica-filled stones of many different mineral colors. For a short while we wade in the creek, tracking it through much thicker vegetation. The creek creates open spaces between the trees, where the sun's rays nurture an immense variety of small plants. Suddenly the creek introduces us to the Hunstein River.

The crystal clear water of the river flows slowly by in a majestic procession of swirls, serenaded by the everlasting drone of cicadas, and draped with flowering red liana vines. The sandbar we once played on, as well as the deep main stream, have shifted to the other side of the small island, testimony to the river's force in its wilder moments. The water looks gold with tiny white crests where it races over shallow sand. It is cool, clean and refreshing. Within minutes it is full of the tired bodies of hikers. Jim and Bahio help us set up our family's gear on the small island.

In the evening, when Rob and I have tucked the children safely in our room-sized tent, we sit around a campfire on the sand bar with Jim, Bahio and a few others, listening to the distant peals of thunder and watching the stars as the clouds flicker with lightning on the horizon. It will rain tonight, as it will almost every night in the Hunstein range, regardless of the time of year. The catfish Ma Jim caught for supper fries over hot coals, warming us for our coming battle with water. Only experience can tell how well our equipment will hold up to a normal, tropical down-pour. Everything has to be put up by our tent on the island and off of the sandbar, as the river will certainly rise with the evening.

Jim and Bahio, honeymooners and full of zest for life, not only become our closest friends, but also our most insightful guides. Their own love for the rainforest leads them to explore and discover many things that others miss. They are fluent communicators in *Tok Pisin*. As Jim relaxes it is apparent that he has mostly outgrown his problem with stuttering.

This ritual of sitting around the campfire together, begun on the sand bar, allows me to get to know a few of the carriers better, but I am well aware that I still do not understand their situation. Improving their circumstances is the key to saving the forest because unless they get some income from somewhere else they will continue to be tempted by loggers. The Bahinemo culture and the Hunstein rainforest are deeply intertwined and the fate of each rests on the other.

During the night, we are fortunate enough to be able to fix the few leaks in our tent with sealant. The tent itself stays up despite stormy winds.

Even when there is no rain, the river goes up several inches every night. My father always thought this was because the steady evaporation which takes place in multitudes of forest leaves was slower at night than during the day. He may have been right. Through the process of transpiration, a rainforest makes its own rain. Scientists estimate that each acre produces 20,000 gallons of water each day.

Damp but not inundated, we arise to a sound like the whistle of fireworks coasting down over our heads. Several hornbills, usually very common in the valley but absent the day before, have come back to see if the expedition has left yet. Spying us, they fly on followed by a flock of white cockatoos, presumably on the same mission.

After lunch, I introduce Gabriel, Sarah and Rob to a family tradition. We head into the forest alone. Our goal is to get to a sand bar upriver and float the currents back down to the camp.

The whole valley is a flood plain where colossal seasonal torrents flush out most of the smaller plants, creating a gallery of giants. Even so, myriads of orchids cling to the sides of trees higher up. Here and there are outstanding examples of what we in the West think of as house plants, only much larger. Some of the buttress roots we wander among are ten feet high and fifteen feet long, creating rooms between the roots. Massive "strangler" vines, some ten inches in diameter, wind their way up trees until one can no longer tell what part of the huge twisted mass is tree and what is vine. Orange and yellow eight-inch leaves drift slowly down from the canopy towering well over a hundred feet above us. The stillness is tangible, holy.

After several minutes, my children get a little anxious that we might become lost so I teach them how to listen to the rise and fall of the cicadas to gauge how far we are from the river. Suddenly, a loud, vigorous clapping sound indicates that we have scared up a Victoria Crowned Pigeon. These beautiful two foot high, blue and purple doves with the tall, exquisite white lace crests are almost extinct elsewhere in the world, but still very common in the Hunstein range. We cut back toward the river and help each other down the mud bank clinging to roots.

In the middle of the river is a sandbar which has snagged a number of large fallen trees. Their scattered conglomeration of twisted roots and limbs now bleached and sanded smooth, make a playground for the children, with balance beams, towers and bouncing animal shapes to ride. Wherever the water swirls around logs in high times, it creates deep crystal clear pools for swimming. What lures me is that it is untouched. There are no footprints but those of the crowned pigeon, no trampled grass. So many treasures-- beautiful stones, driftwood, and exotic flowers, fruits and seeds--lay wherever they have fallen, pristine.

The expedition, made up of fifteen different scientists and their assistants and carriers, is establishing itself at four stops along the way up the mountain's shoulder. They have given up reaching the top of the mountain itself, with the exception of biologist Dr. Allison and his personal guide. Each group follows its own agenda. We catch up with the botanists at Gipa, otherwise known as "Camp Two."

To get to Gipa we must follow the Hunstein River around the second of the two ridges that separate Wagu from Mt. Hunstein. Most of the trail takes us on soft mud under the forest canopy, but there are nine river crossings. After a while, the sandy bottom of the lower river gives way to fast cold water and slippery rocks. The air cools to about 75 degrees. We stop and pass out crackers and cheese to all those hiking with us. Each time we step out into the bright, noon sun to cross the river, we marvel at blue swallows and iridescent blue, yellow and purple butterflies flickering and dancing back and forth across the wide rapids. The river seems to be a ravine as dense vegetation on both banks rises from the ground to the top of the canopy.

Several low bunk houses made of clear plastic over sapling frames comprise Camp Two, or Gipa, which is hidden in the trees. In front of the camp is a wide expanse of large rocks stretching far out into the river. To my delight, the camp also features a well-dug outhouse. There is a large crowd of Bahinemo carriers along with some Papua New Guinea scientists at Gipa. We settle into one of the bunk houses and start a fire for supper. Just up-stream is a crystal clear pool of water ideal for swimming. Again, the scene is decorated with red flowers from "Flame of the Forest" lianas. The water is chilly but welcome after the day's hike.

Here is our grand introduction to kauri pines, apparently the "gold" of timber industries. On the side of the river which faces the camp, a steep ridge rises, and along that ridge they stand like grand sentinels, head and shoulders above all other trees. Close inspection reveals perfect symmetrical, round trunks with diameters of three to four feet. The trees stand about 150 feet tall, rising straight up off the sloping ground and piercing the canopy like needles through cloth. They are what the logging companies seek.

We barely get settled in that first night in Gipa, when a tremendous deluge of water breaks down onto the camp. Water falls in buckets, and workers hurry to empty parts of the plastic roofs which are not quite taut enough to resist a buildup of 40 to 60 pounds of water in only a few minutes. Soon all of the ground is soaked with two or three inches of swirling water. The river rises above the field of stones and approaches its banks.

Some of the Americans in the party worry that our camp will flood as the river rises to the brink of the bank. However, the Bahinemos remain sound asleep on the ground only a few feet from the swirling current.

Those who awaken because of the clamor laugh, "This is just an ordinary rain."

"If it rained like this for three days in a row then we would worry," Ma Lekim explains. It is part of the predictable rhythm of the forest that the river is dug just deep enough to hold the normal amount of water it needs to carry a standard size rain. If an unusually long rain happened, streams hidden in the forest would be activated before any true flooding occurred.

"The water is still clear!" exclaims Dr. Sohmer. "This *is* a healthy rainforest. It is still completely balanced." He explains to me that even slight disturbances of a rainforest allow the soil to wash away. In this one, the numerous plants still hold it all in place.

The watershed is the most important reason for preserving this type of forest. The soil in tropical rainforests is very thin, and without roots to hold it together it will wash away, leaving bare rock which cannot grow anything. Once that happens the climate begins to dry out, with no trees to produce moisture and no soil to hold it. Droughts occur. When it does rain, the water rushes straight off the barren land, creating floods of muddy water such as the ones in Bangladesh, the result of forests cut down on the Himalayas.

Our family has left our large tent at Bani. We snuggle securely in individual army jungle hammocks set up as tents on a bark platform under plastic tarps. The rain streams over the clear plastic above our heads but we are dry and comfortable. Listening to its soft rhythmic tapping takes me back to my childhood once again and sleep comes easily. In the morning the river returns to normal.

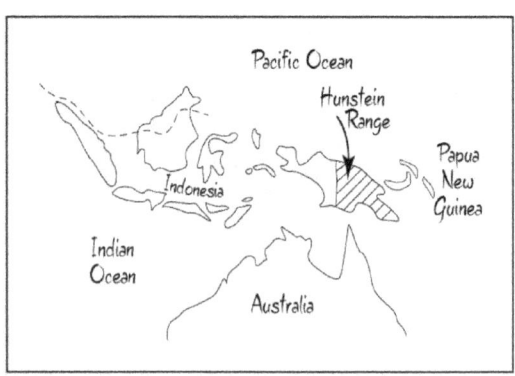

Chapter 4

The Cold Places

~~ Mommy played in one pool after
another. She said the little bugs that danced
in the pools were fairies. We called our falls
Fairy Falls and went back again and again to
swim in its pools. The pools were beautiful
and each was higher than the last, separated
by a tiny waterfall. We followed the pools a
long way up. One day Mommy started
screaming and running. Daddy said wasps
were in her hair. ~~

On my second night in Gipa, I overhear some complaints in
the plastic bunkhouse where the Bahinemos sleep. It seems the camp
supervisor denied two men a normal allotment of rice and canned
mackerel. They had tagged along, but were never officially hired.
Since the two men were not allowed to eat, all the carriers refuse to
eat. The supervisor is a Papua New Guinean. Because of the large
crowd following us, he has implemented the policy that only those
hired on a salary basis could stay in camp and receive meals. The
carriers, however, do not understand this. It's their land. They can't
comprehend being encouraged to leave or being left out of group
meals. I advise the supervisor to hire and feed all who are present.

The next day more trouble brews, this time with talk of
abandoning the camp. Westerners, terrified of being left stranded in
the forest alone, call this "carrier mutiny."

"How is it that one man works hard all day carrying a heavy
unwieldy pack, while another sits around all day doing nothing, and
they both get the same amount of pay?" the carriers ask me. I have
to explain what it is like to live in a town in order to explain the
system of weekly salaries. This idea confuses the carriers. They
have no idea what it would be like to depend on a steady income.
Without that understanding, the system does appear quite unfair.

I am confident that this entire expedition is doing everything it can to accommodate the carriers' every need. How would these same men cope with a commercial company whose priorities would not include their welfare? Clearly if any outside company did come into the Hunstein range, there would be a host of cultural conflicts.

I spend the next few days getting my family acclimated to the surrounding area. I am fighting a sore throat with antibiotics so Jay goes on up the trail ahead of me with a few of the carriers.

The children love the rocks and the water, as well as the scenery, but they are not fond of the giant, biting flies and other strange, ever present bugs. On the second night we find a cockroach in our camp that is so large we can't kill it by pounding it with rocks. Finally the scientists catch it and pop it into a collection jar. It must be about five or six inches long.

Nevertheless the children settle quickly and are especially delighted one day to discover that Ma Jim, who had previously kept this a secret, speaks English. San Bahio is doing her very best to teach them how to fish and Jim builds a tree house with vines in a matter of hours. There are also a few other children along to play with and soon I find Sarah sharing a string hammock with another child, both engrossed in examining each other's hair for lice. Sarah doesn't have lice, but I am glad to see her joining in with one of their common pastimes.

Rob and I go on an excursion of our own. Hidden in the ridge opposite the camp is a cave into which pounds a twenty-foot waterfall. After swimming for a while in its deep, golden glow we decide to find out where the light that makes the glow comes from. Groping our way along the side of the ridge, we find a tiny crevice in the rock wall. We squeeze through and discover that it leads directly above where the water falls into the cave.

There above is another falls, and above that another and another, each creating a Jacuzzi sized pool in which to play. We go up and up until we tire of our explorations and come back down to tell the camp of our discovery.

Suddenly out of nowhere, a huge lightning bolt strikes the middle of the camp. This is followed immediately by a completely unanticipated deluge which inundates the camp and then stops as quickly as it began.

The camp is a buzz of whispers as news spreads of our adventure. Apparently the creek is cursed, a dead warrior having been thrown into it years before. The Bahinemos blame Rob and me for the lightning and the deluge and consider us lucky to be alive.

While in Gipa, I get to watch Wayne Takiuchi and the other scientists from the Wau Ecology Institute laying out transepts. They mark out a certain distance of forest in a straight line with a string, then measure and describe every tree within so many feet on either side of it. Much later they will do the same thing on the exact same spot to determine such things as the growth rate of certain types of trees in the area. Each night the men also bring back bags of flowers and leaves which they soak in alcohol and pack to be sent off to various museums.

It is time for me to go on alone to the next camp, leaving Rob, Gabriel and Sarah in Gipa. I see no need for them to follow me deeper into the unknown. Bahio and Jim will take good care of them. I must visit each of the scientist's camps to write about their discoveries. I kiss my family goodbye and set out up the trail with two Bahinemo companions.

My guides and carriers are Ma Lekim and Ma Gogomo. Ma Lekim's Western name is Solomon. I always call Solomon "Ma Lekim" and he often calls me "San Lekim", because he is my uncle, having adopted my father as his brother in a ceremony which involves the tying of vines. "Lekim" means tied vines. That is how I came to be a member of the tribe. Although he is my uncle, he treats me like his own daughter. Ma Gogomo is the village pastor. He is very vivacious and strong. I trust them both with my life, and they make good walking companions. Together we walk along the river to the west, farther into its source until we come to the base of a ridge where we head south, deeper into rainforest.

The forest is so calm and beautiful. Every now and then we hear water trickling or gurgling in the background, in addition to the ongoing melody of birds. I am in awe over the many types of fruits and flower petals which are scattered over our path. Some fruits look like purple rubber balls. Others look like Christmas tree lights or little pink bells. Flowers come in scarlet brushes and long yellow flutes.

Occasionally large hornbills grunt, scold and beat the air with their wings as they gather fruit from the tops of the trees. Now and then we catch a glimpse of one of their three-foot long bodies in handsome black and white dress, or we see the golden head of a male as he plays about in the treetops like a monkey.

We can tell there are wild boars around from their furrows, and cassowaries from their scat. Cassowaries are dangerous, as they are rather foolish and would just as soon run toward you as from you when cornered, but it's hard to corner anything in an open forest, so we aren't worried. When Gogomo gets ahead, he sees one of the large birds on the trail in front of him. It is about five feet tall, rather like an ostrich with a rainbow colored neck and a jade green crown. It runs away before Ma Lekim and I can catch up.

All the way to the ridge, Ma Lekim tells me about the different trails which crisscross the valley. Such trails are not true paths, but rather known routes, such as ridge points and creeks. The trails themselves disappear weeks after people use them. Ma Lekim is now passing knowledge of these routes down to me in the same manner as his ancestors passed it down to him.

As we climb the ridge to the south, the forest gradually becomes less humid, though it never actually dries up. We are now beyond the normal hunting range, and so we often come across enormous trees which the Bahinemo would fell for canoes if they were closer to the village. One could envision the Swiss Family Robinson in such trees, which brings back childhood fantasies of hiding in the rainforest forever.

As we pass one tree, Ma Gogomo slashes off a small piece of bark with his machete. "Here. Smell this," he says. It smells like allspice. Soon he also finds a cinnamon tree. There are many such trees, he assures me.

We have hiked well into the afternoon when a waft of cool air blows down from the mountain top. Ma Lekim says, "We have reached the cold places," with much awe in his voice. From here on, the ground is perpetually moist. I am amazed to find there is virtually no soil at all. Instead, masses of tangled roots, mosses and large and small plants cling together holding the moisture for each other. Underneath, water drips over bare rock. Indeed if something happened to the trees, no one could ever replant here.

Ma Lekim and Ma Gogomo start a heated conversation about our route as they stop to shift their loads. They claim that the scientists who went before us cut the trail up the wrong ridge, this one being much steeper and more out of the way than the route further up the valley. "Why didn't they listen to me?" Ma Lekim asks. "Now the expedition might not ever reach the summit".

"Woa, woa, woa," rises a loud, forceful cry from above, in higher and higher notes. It is the famous bird-of-paradise. We stop and stare until we catch a glimpse of its luxurious golden plumage flitting around in the trees.

Very late in the afternoon, we arrive at Camp Three. A member of the first party called it "Twenty Mile" after feeling like the party had walked that far since Gipa. We had probably only covered three or four miles as the crow flies, but it took hours.

I find a place to hang my screen jungle hammock, equipped with its own roof. Then I put my bowl and fork along with everyone else's on the sapling table for a helping of rice and mackerel. I am the only woman here and I am desperate for a bath. While I rarely smell sweat on Bahinemo bodies, mine is American and I need to rinse off. I go a little ways from camp alone. I am frightened in the dusk and not sure where all the men are as I take a very cold rinse in a tiny creek. The foliage is unfamiliar, adding to my angst.

Back at camp, I burn my hand over the steaming kettle and it hurts. However talk about the myths of the mountain distracts me as the carriers and I gather around the campfire and eat.

The Bahinemos believe only one group of people have walked this far on the mountain before. It was a group of scientists called the CSIRO whom the Australian government had sent in 1966. I had tackled the other side of the mountain with my family as a teenager after a two day trip up the remote April River. The Germans claimed to have gone to the top during their occupation before the First World War. No one knows for sure whether they made it or which way they went. No one knows if anyone has ever reached the true summit.

Some of the men and I can remember the CSIRO trip from our childhoods. Many amazing stories formed out of those memories.

"They hired my older brother", one of the carriers says, "and thereafter he became rich!"

"My mother always said, 'Just wait, son. Someday the white men will want to find the mountain again and then you will be rich too!'" Much laughter comes from the carriers at this. Here he is, and he is certainly not getting rich from it.

"They had huge pots of rice to eat every night," another says.

"It was so cold the skin fell off of the bottom of many of the men's feet," two men warn. I remember the thorny vines that carpeted the trail from the expedition when I was a teenager, and how those thorns slashed even my dog's feet to shreds. Several nod their heads, relieved when I offer this as the explanation for that myth.

"That expedition was when you encountered the type of cassowary that attacks people," one man reminds us.

Wayne, the main scientist for this camp, promptly calls these "kung-fu cassowaries." We have all been watching for the smaller mountain version of cassowary which the people believe to be fiercer. I remember the one which had run right into our camp on my previous expedition. I thought perhaps it had never seen humans before and didn't know to stay away. If it was frightened, or cornered between us and the steep mountain, it might indeed have attacked.

We all just laugh about the stories of the giant tree kangaroos that eat dogs.

Someone fills the rice pot with water and we make tea over the fire and talk about how to keep warm. I have hung my hammock in a tree for privacy instead of stretching it out in the men's shelter, but I soon regret this. Even with a space blanket wrapped around me in the night, I feel like a block of ice, as do the Bahinemos with no blankets at all.

Cold is what prevented the Bahinemos from ever making an expedition of their own past the edge of cloud forest, characterized by cold, dense fog and thick mounds of moss. Traditionally they had no way of coping with nightly temperatures of around 40 degrees Fahrenheit since they wore almost no clothing. A change in temperature of more than 10 degrees is a rare phenomenon which they fear. Cold would keep them awake and exposed to the bizarre mountain night. At least this time they are wearing clothes.

Inside the forest, in the dark, it is difficult to tell whether one is right side up or upside down. A fungus which glows in the dark is scattered over both the tree trunks and the ground, causing them to light up as much or more than the tropical stars hidden in the leafy canopy overhead.

Hundreds of frogs with a shocking array of voices cry out. They sound like everything from creaky doorways to computer watch alarms, or baby goats. An owl sounds like a woman screaming. Every few minutes the cry of one of the many types of bats fills the air, breaking the cacophony of the frogs with a sound that I can only describe as shattering crystal glass. All night long I keep hearing an eerie thump, thump, pounding around the camp. I dream that I have strung my hammock right across the "kung-fu cassowary's" trail.

Red liana flowers close up

Hunstein River near Gipa

Chapter 5

Compromises and Exploitation

*~~I hung on to the tow rope for dear life,
straining to hold my body in the perfect position.
Finally I was up on top of the water. Waterskiing
is something like flying and I flew all around the
lake. The cool breeze was such a relief from the
humid tropics that I didn't care when I scared up
birds as I zoomed by.*

*With a pang of guilt I later realized we
missionaries had used up more fuel waterskiing
than the village church needed for a whole
mission trip they were going to cancel for lack of
funds. This took the fun out of waterskiing for me
from then on.~~*

A few of us head for the highest camp early in the morning.
My companions and I have caught up with Jay. Both Jay and I are
eager to find Dr. Allison and Debby and Andy, his two American
interns. Dr. Allison is taking a vertebrate survey while Debby and
Andy collect birds. The three of them have proven to be as elusive
as their prey. Until now, each time I arrived at one of their camps
they had deliberately moved on first thing in the morning or even
the night before, fearing the additional number of carriers I have
hired for my family would hinder their collecting. I wonder if I will
finally see them today.

The calls of exotic birds-of-paradise, Palm cockatoos and
brightly colored parrots fill the air. We see large birds landing in
nearby trees regularly. As the trail follows the ridge, it advances
steeply both up and down.

For several hours we continue on along the ridge, savoring
the isolation, the absolute untouched wilderness, the quiet stillness
and the endless green, when suddenly we come across a blond and
bearded man. It's Andy, checking traps. A few minutes later we
meet Debbie who, as though we have all been together for some

time, asks without any greeting, "Have you seen Andy?" Then she hurries on past. We have arrived.

Camp Four is a disappointment to me, being quite a bit more primitive than the others. The scientists have thrown together a make-shift shelter covered with plastic which nearly collapses when touched. I quickly learn rule number one: Don't touch anything! The camp is small and crowded compared with the other camps, but offers a fantastic view.

Debbie and Andy have set up a bench on the edge of the ridge to watch birds. It looks out over a vast and untouched valley and more mountains. On the map these mountains are blotted by white spaces marked "obscured by cloud," which indeed they are. Our own perch on the side of the mountain is also almost always in cloud.

It drizzles all day, every day, and rains every night. This explains the several feet of moss which cover both the ground and the trees. The trees are thick, though they seem to cling only to the moss and each other's roots. The constant drizzle also accounts for the vast variety of frogs present both day and night.

Dr. Allison is busy preserving a type of rat when we first arrive in the high camp. Without looking up from his work, he mutters, "Put your sleeping bags in the empty shelter." Then, looking only at Jay, he stoically answers my questions about his finds. I never find out what he has against me, the journalist. Despite this outward lack of enthusiasm or social finesse, he is quite knowledgeable and excited about frogs. He has discovered what he hopes are several new species. He has also made recordings of frog songs. "Each variety of frog has its own song and it chooses the right mate out of all the many, many species present, just by following that correct song," he explains to Jay.

At night I watch Debbie and Andy meticulously stuff their catch of birds for the day. They handle them mercifully but I am still somewhat horrified. It is a necessary evil in order to bring back proof of which birds exist in the region. How many more compromises might be necessary in order to preserve the rainforest? What choices would the Bahinemos face in the process of trying to save their land and their culture?

Debbie and Andy are ecstatic over a rare shovel-billed kingfisher. Two female birds of paradise are in the day's catch with the nets but by now these are getting to be routine.

While they haven't discovered any new species of birds, the couple are delighted to find that many birds which are rare or even absent in other places are thriving and very common here. Harpy eagles, exotic gold and azure kingfishers, unusual birds of paradise, and many other national treasures are as common as starlings in the U.S. "Birds which require seasonal migration from one altitude to another may find their entire range right here on this mountain," Debbie explains.

I long to go clear to the summit of Mount Hunstein the next day but everyone informs me that it is very far away. Only Dr. Allison and his assistant claim to have made the trip, and it took them from before dawn until after dark walking very fast. Anyway, it rains all the next day and no one else seems anxious or even willing to join me. Instead, I go with a PNG scientist to help check nets and trap lines.

Harry Sakulas, a Papua New Guinean, is the director of Wau Ecology Institute, a non-governmental organization which tries to encourage alternatives to deforestation. He knows the legal system regarding logging in Papua New Guinea and I want to learn what he knows.

"The first thing that happens when the government discovers the potential for logging is the Forestry Department takes a registry of who owns the land and where their boundaries are. To do this they have to make a recording of the local tribal clan system. Then these true recorded landowners will be given the proposal to log. It's their choice. They can log it, keep it for their own hunting and gathering, or even allot it to be a wildlife preserve."

It sounds so simple.

"The people have a lot of options," Harry continues. "They can, for example, agree to lease the land provided certain permanent roads are built to their village, or provided a hospital is built. The clans can also create their own rules for any area they decide to protect. For instance, they could say, 'we will only allow boar hunting in this section, and only by members of our tribe.' Whatever rules they create will become law, enforceable by the police. To prevent poaching, the landowners themselves must be solidly behind whatever they create. No one could enforce any other park system."

"But how will the villagers know what to do?" I ask. "Multi-national, money hungry corporations will offer life-time salaries and rags-to-riches guarantees in exchange for logging. How will the villagers know how important it is to preserve the forest when they have never been without it?"

Harry sidesteps my question, "An even worse problem is the wording of the contracts. How many landowners speak English well enough to know the legal terms needed to carry out their desires? You can't imagine how clever these multi-national companies can be at re-interpreting contracts."

"So what happens if this territory is so precious that it is an international treasure, or at least a national one? Can the country afford to leave its entire fate in the hands of a few hundred people?"

"Is it so precious?" Harry replies. "That is the point of this expedition. If what we find here is so unique that it would be a terrible shame for the country or the world to lose it forever, then the PNG government could overrule the usual system. But the province needs money and they get 25% of the profits from logging. Also the villagers may or may not co-operate with such a ruling.

"It's a tough situation," he continues. "The government created the land-ownership system for a lot of important reasons. The Hunstein rainforest project is a prototype for the rest of the nation. This is the first time anyone has tried this new system. If we can, we need to work within it."

Heavy shadows on the dripping vegetation say it is time to return to camp. As I follow the trail back through the leaves and deep moss, savoring the last whispering bird-calls for the day, the trees around me await their fate, prisoners in a holding cell. Only they are more innocent than babes.

On the way back to camp I think of a situation already occurring in the village where the villagers are being manipulated. While we were in Wagu the week before, I had been invited to a rather dismal birthing scene. A woman had given birth to a small frail baby who was having a lot of trouble breathing.

"You need to hold this baby," I admonished the mother sitting morosely on the cold cement floor, staring at the wall. The baby was losing body temperature fast. The mother had given up on it the moment it produced a faint, gurgled cry, and both she and the midwife had left it lying on the wet, bloody cement floor. I picked it up, wrapped it in tin foil and tucked mother and child together on a pallet of cloth. With a simple bulb syringe I cleared its breathing passages.

The village doctor came and gave the mother five aspirins to take all at once. I cringed as I wondered what this might do to the already weak baby through the mother's milk. Then he gave the situation a cursory glance and left.

In the morning I was relieved to hear the baby crying normally.

It was a situation that had repeated itself in Wagu village too many times. Whooping cough, preventable by vaccination, was also rampant in the village. Diseases of every kind seem to have increased. I heard complaints:

"This doctor is never available when we need him."

"He doesn't tell anyone how to reach him when he goes away."

"He doesn't give injections the right way. He gives adult doses to children."

"Ma Mufan and San Bogo have lost three out of four babies," one young woman lamented to me in secret. "Both of Watabu's babies died; her first-born and her second. They laughed and played on her lap one day, and the very next, they died."

Some villagers, however, including 60 year old Ma Lekim, defended the doctor with fervor. "The doctor? He's a good doctor. He's not at fault," Ma Lekim said, when I asked him about the doctor's care as we walked along the trail together. "These young girls aren't taking care of their children like our generation of women used to. They take them in the sun. That's what's wrong." I asked him about vaccinations and he shrugged and replied, "That's something only doctors know about. I don't know anything about that."

Most of the Bahinemos whom I asked about the doctor told me to leave the subject alone. But Ma Jim confided in me that the whole village was afraid that if anyone reported anything negative about the doctor, the government might take him away and never replace him, leaving them all medically destitute. Ma Lekim admitted this was true.

Meanwhile the doctor had demanded that two large houses be built for him. He had padlocked the community water tank for his own use, leaving the villagers to drink from the dysentery-infected stream. And he had introduced drunken brawls and modern dance nights for the young people, breaking up family traditions, and causing the village's first problem with alcohol. He had accomplished all of this by telling the people that one complaint would make him leave and no one would replace him.

Sometimes he left for a week just to prove his point.

Just thinking about it all again, fills me with rage at so much abuse. It makes me feel so helpless. Yet all was due to the simple but selfish manipulation of just one man. How many more ways could sophisticated profit conscious developers with greater prizes in mind find to use the naiveté of the people, than this somewhat educated man from one village away?

I find Camp Four rather eerie. Strong preserving chemicals and bags containing the last dying leaps and cries of formaldehyde soaked frogs surround me. It is a bit unsettling. I suppose if I didn't have a natural revulsion to killing animals for any reason, I would never have cared so much about the situation to start with. The outside world has to have an official record of what lives on Hunstein Mountain, and word of mouth is apparently just not official enough. I resolve myself to the collecting. Perhaps the few can save the many.

On my second night in camp, Dr. Allison and Jay leave to hunt for frogs. The gruesome task of skinning birds thoroughly engrosses Debbie and Andy. It is pitch black due to the ever surrounding clouds, except for the ghostly clumps of glowing fungus. On my way to get dressed for bed, my flashlight dies.

I feel around to try to find my batteries in the shed, momentarily forgetting the "don't touch anything" rule. "Crash!"

There goes one end of the shelter. Knowing Dr. Allison has hung some sort of specimens to dry at that end, I edge carefully through the inches deep mud to check out the damage I have done. In the dark I feel a box laying on its side full of...Ugh! Little skeletons and bats! I do my best not to scream, and try to figure out who to turn to for help without getting myself in more trouble.

I don't find anybody. Somehow I manage to arrange my sleeping bag and get in bed. I doze off.

"Boooom!"

A shotgun splits the night two feet from our beds. The carriers have killed a pair of Silky Phalangers. They are very soft and cuddly possums with big, round eyes and bunny rabbit fur, not at all reminiscent of rat-like American opossums.

Inside the pouch of the female is a tiny baby, still alive. I snatch her from the scientists' hands, where she is destined for a pickle jar and tuck her into my pocket. I leave the camp at first light before they can take her from me. I name her Angelina Samsai or "Little Angel of Mount Hunstein."

This precious surprise delights Sarah when after two days of hiking down I arrive back in Gipa. I have baby animal formula waiting for just such an occasion and Angelina is soon thriving on it.

Back in Gipa I become known as the "Squeamish Doctor". The carriers form long lines to wait for my impromptu medical clinic. I am not, in fact, a doctor, but growing up in the village taught me to handle most rainforest situations and I must bandage deep cuts with antibiotics and vitamin E as well as diagnose the occasional malarial patient, whom I send home.

Each time I encounter a gross wound, I make a big deal about how awful it looks and how I don't want to look at it, let alone get near it to clean it with iodine. This makes the line of carriers howl with laughter. There are many such wounds and my evening "clinic" usually lasts a fun filled hour after we tuck the kids into their nets.

When we get downriver to Bani again, we have our belongings unloaded on the island where we slept on the way up. The Bahinemos are dismayed to find that we prefer to sleep on the island again instead of on the higher cleared bank as it has been raining longer and more often. But I anticipate there might be fewer chiggers on the shaded tree covered island and insist.

After some deliberation, Ma Lekim declares we may set up our large tent there, but only if we allow the carriers to build us a high platform for our tents in case of high water. We are soon astonished to see them haul in about fifty 3 and 4 inch diameter trees to create a floor. It's another compromise.

"Must you really cut down so many trees?" I exclaim, trying to act grateful for their efforts but feeling dismayed. "We could still move to the other bank, rather than have you cut so much."

They laugh. "There are thousands and thousands of trees where they came from, San Edie. Stop worrying so much." That night I am ensconced on a castle of frivolous waste. I am wrong about the chiggers. I don't think I have ever felt so many bites.

It pours for several hours each night. The first night, the river rises ten feet. At noon we have a fresh, clean sandbar and stream again. On the second night the water almost covers the island. These are normal affairs for the rainforest. It is very frightening, however, to look out on the swirling river beneath our platform in the dark.

I think a lot about what Dr. Sy Sohmer said about the primary concern being the watershed. The entire village of Wagu depends on the watershed of this one river. Losing the rainforest would destroy the lifestyle of the village. But do they know that?

On the way back to Wagu I am acutely aware that the lake has changed. When I grew up in Wagu village, the lake was a living storehouse of plenty. Large pink lotus lilies along the edge of the marsh filled the air with their sweet fragrance. Smaller blue lilies with delicious edible stems and seed pods, and swarms of ducks, fish and birds, filled it with life from shore to shore.

Then tragedy struck. Someone dumped imported plants out of their fish aquarium into a Sepik waterway. With no enemies, the salvinia weed spread. Within months, it covered virtually all of the lakes, rivers, ponds and still-water streams in the whole Sepik province. It gathered in mounds three feet thick killing lilies, fish, birds and people. Some people got caught in its grasp while coming home from fishing and died. Others starved to death because they couldn't go out to the forest in their canoes or catch fish. In a year or two, after much research and effort, the wildlife department introduced a bug that ate salvinia. The waterways cleared, but now the lake lay barren.

The lilies are gone. Floating dead fish cover the lake in the dry season. Perhaps they cannot find solace from the heat among the missing lilies. Birds on the lake are scarce compared to the past. I don't see ducks. The lake seems dead. I am devastated at the power of one little foreign species. But the fragility of a lake doesn't begin to compare with the delicate, vulnerable complexity of a rainforest. I wonder just how much change the rainforest could handle without falling apart.

It's hard to believe our time in the rainforest is over.

Back in the village, we settle into a routine with the kids alternately playing with Ma Jim and San Bahio and following Grandma around. My mother makes elaborate meals and I am especially enjoying our standard breakfast of papaya, pineapple and banana salad, oatmeal, toast and coffee.

Poor Jay misses out on these delights for a few days, though. He comes down with a violent attack of malaria or some sort of flu rumored to cause death. He is ready to demand a helicopter out when he finally gets well.

One day I notice some women have a mouse-like creature with a long, pointy nose crawling around in their string bag.

"What will you do with it?" I ask.

"Oh, it will soon die. It's just a baby," they reply.

"Then may I keep it?" I ask, tucking it into my shirt to warm it up. It's a bandicoot and it's the ugliest creature I have ever seen, with its spiky fur and web like feet, beady eyes and long pointy nose. Rob and I promptly name him Beasty.

Soon I itch like crazy. The baby has given me lice.

Fortunately a routine supply trip to Ambunti produces a bar of anti-flea soap and I bathe both myself and the little creature.

Beasty and Angelina are soon eating fruit in addition to lapping earnestly at their pet milk. I am used to raising small animals and can practically see the two of them growing. Beasty is the strangest creature I have ever raised. He spends his time rooting through our sheets with his nose.

Angelina, the Silky Phalanger

Beastie, the baby bandicoot

Chapter 6

Village in Conflict

~~ *"What are you eating?" the man
asked my parents in the 1960s.*

*"We are eating canned fruit," they
answered bemused at the never ending list of
strange questions the Bahinemo people thought to
ask about their lifestyle.*

*"No you are not," the man replied. "I can
clearly see that you are eating babies. See there is
a picture of a baby on the can."* ~~

"The territory of the clan of the moon and the sun, it looks to
me like this," describes Ma Kitu, barely audible with his voice
hoarse from a recent night of singing. He is trying to explain what
part of the Hunstein Forest his clan owns. But he has never thought
to describe it before and has no idea how to explain the boundaries.

"You start at the place where we yell out at the Yambi
Yambi people, and go this way to that place. Follow the mountain to
Yambi Yambi. Then follow the edge of the mountain until you get
to that river. Okay. Then you cut along the side of the mountain,
along the border of the clan of the cassowary. Follow their border
and then turn back again. Go to the path where we used to get
lycees. Come this way again a little ways and you'll get to the top.
Go to the other side and follow the water down part way."

The law says the landowners get to decide what happens to
their forest. Various clans own different parts of the forest so the
village has called a meeting to sort things out and clarify which land
belongs to whom.

Suddenly people are coming from all over the world to see
the Bahinemos' land. "What will happen to us? What are our rights?
What will we gain from all this?" The villagers wonder. The

Forestry Department gives them the impression that they will replace every piece of forest which is cut down. This is a complete misunderstanding of the concept of "replanting" which can only produce a garden of trees, not a rainforest.

I want to teach the Bahinemos about the true effect of logging on rainforests. But I must wait until I understand their point of view. If what I say sounds too foolish or farfetched, I might lose their confidence. For them this is all as though some aliens came down and wanted to buy their sky. Why not sell it? What harm could they possibly do to it? I am frustrated. I want to scream out what will happen to their culture and lifestyle if they lose the forest. But I would have to tell what I know in steps that make sense to their different world view. I am still not confident as to how that way of thinking works. As a *National Geographic* reporter I am not supposed to get involved, just observe. As a woman I would not get respect. The job of telling the Bahinemos about saving the trees will have to fall to someone else, but who? If only I had time to learn to communicate the effects that deforestation would have on the village, let alone the loss for the world; reporter, woman or not, I would.

The meeting is full of men, but the women want to hear as well, so they sit at the edge of the gathering with their children who cry or yell. Dogs wander through the group and yelp away when clobbered, or howl in unison over some crisis of their own. Roosters crow. Everyone keeps talking past everyone else.

Representatives of the forestry department and the local government had arrived a few days earlier to register the names of landowners. Unfortunately, on that day most of the village elders went out hunting. Younger men and people who were not true landowners gave the department incorrect names, signing their own names in places of advantage. Having recorded the "landowners", the officials promise to be back soon to record the boundaries.

When the older men learned what happened, uproar ensued. They will have to send an appeal to the government to amend the name list. They decide to define all correct boundaries immediately before the officials take any more records. Hence the meeting. This turns out to be a most difficult task, however. Perhaps it is the first time anyone has been called upon to describe their land in words: "You go up the hill to the malay apple trees. Then you follow the creek toward the wild boar trail…"

I can't resist getting involved any longer. I acquire a topographical map from the mission at Ambunti and enlarge it section by section until I have a six foot square map of the whole 600 square mile Hunstein range. I show them how to record their borders on the map. We also present a copy of the fraudulently registered names so the elders can correct it. Without these interventions, it is doubtful the Bahinemos could accurately register the land of their clans.

As the picture of the clans and their boundaries begins to unfold, we realize some very significant dynamics of saving the forest. All of the land from Wagu to the top of Mount Hunstein, including everything the expedition covered, belonged to one man named Yalfei, who has recently died.

At one time, a small group in the Hunstein rainforest attacked a village on the Sepik River. The men were ambushed and killed, leaving a teenage boy named Yalfei and the women. Most of the woman ran far away, but the teenage boy and a few of the women stayed on. Yalfei went to other small groups in the forest and invited them onto the land that had been left vacant on the lake. They built some houses, and called the place Wagu. From Kagiru, a man named Kudul joined them with his wives and eight kids. As Yalfei grew older he fell in love with the Kudul's eldest daughter named Moyali and they were happily married.

A generous and gentle leader, Yalfei continued the history of inviting others to live and hunt on his land. He and Moyali also raised many foster kids over the years, having only one daughter of their own. At last, shortly before Yalfei passed away, he had a son: the sole heir to all of the Tuhiyu land. His name is Mathew.

As Mathew is just a young child, his mother, San Moyali, makes all the decisions for the time being, regarding the clan and its members. It is almost unheard of for a woman to have a job as important as hers. She controls Wagu Lake, the Hunstein River, Mount Hunstein, and all the land in between including the watershed from the mountain to the lake. In a way, she is the head of Wagu village.

I am sitting at the table after dinner going over the map when I notice Moyali and her daughter, Wama, watching me shyly through the screen door. I invite them to come in. "Would you like to look at the map?" I ask.

"No", she replies, "I am hoping Rob can fix my radio." My husband takes a look at it. Someone has switched the power setting from DC to AC.

Content once her radio is fixed, Moyali turns to leave, but we call her to go over the map with us one more time, this time on her own. It turns out she has never seen a map up close and doesn't realize what it is. We show her the rivers, the sago swamps, the mountains, the hunting grounds and the boundaries we have drawn on the map. Then I try to explain to her that her land covers the entire watershed and resource area for the whole village. I point out that her decision alone will decide the fate of the land the village lives off of for all of their children and their children's children. She nods solemnly.

We go on to other subjects. She comments on how attached my children are to their grandparents. "Yes," I say, "After this week, who knows when they will see them next. Mom and Dad are going to Africa, you know. I haven't ever been to Africa. It's not like America where we usually go. It's a completely different place, quite far from the U.S. or PNG I've only seen it in pictures."

"I understand completely," she replies."I too have never seen Inaro or Begabuki. They are very far away. I only hear about them." She refers to the nearest tribes to the South. The farthest boundaries of her world reach only to Ambunti and the neighboring tribes, each a distance of about 20 miles away.

Two days later, when the leaders of the village have made most of the corrections to the registry of clan members, I am concerned to see there are still several different versions going around regarding who is in Moyali's clan. Two outsiders, Andrew and the present doctor are both registered as members. I wonder if she really understands the purpose and significance of the registry.

"Who is really supposed to belong in your clan?" I ask Moyali directly when we are alone. "Me, my daughter and Mathew," She replies. "We are the leaders."

"Is there anyone else?"

"No. We're the last ones. Well yes, two of my foster sons have rights. I've unofficially adopted Seqedi and Weseli but they remain under us in order of rights."

"Are you quite sure that is all who should be on the list?" I ask again.

"Yes, quite sure. Those are all who have rights to this land."

"Well," I ask judiciously. "What about Andrew and the doctor, the two men from down the Sepik River? They put their names on your list as well; and also Waga, who comes from a clan on the other side of the mountain."

"Ah yes, that's right," she sighs. "They all want to be in it as well, so that makes three more families."

Does she realize she is giving them more than living space this time? Does she realize that by being in her clan they get to decide what happens to Hunstein forest too?

I try to think of a way to help San Moyali understand the critical nature of the decisions which she's required to make. These outsiders she is allowing in could completely take control of the whole process and they don't care about the culture or the forest.

"What if you die and your kids die too? Who would you want to take over the leadership of your clan?" I ask.

"My foster kids," she replies.

Moyali is uncomfortable with this turn of the discussion so I repeatedly assure her it is all just talk. Talking about this doesn't mean she is going to die. Speculation is a new concept.

"If something terrible happened to them too, then who would it be?" I press again.

"Well, then it would go to Ma Kenyafo, the leader of the clan of the Hornbill."

This is not what the registry says.

"Should it not go to Andrew, or the doctor, or perhaps Waga?" I ask, puzzled at the inconsistency.

"Certainly not!" she exclaims. "They are outsiders. We can't give them our land, they can only use it."

Government law states that only true clan members can register land, not outsiders. Only officially adopted people can be clan members. A true family member will usually act in the best interest of the whole family regarding land jurisdiction. An outsider, particularly if he is more educated, can easily manipulate real owners into serving his own interests. The doctor is already an example of this. By allowing these outside families into her clan, Moyali is giving them and their descendants a share in the control over the Hunstein forest. They have no cultural or historical ties to the forest. They could survive quite well with an urban lifestyle, enjoying the financial gains of logging, while she and her true kin would find the loss of their rainforest devastating.

I explain the law to San Moyali, but am unable to convey the possible consequences. She makes no move to take the outsiders off the list.

"If I don't include some of these others on my land, I will be all alone here, and I can't survive all by myself," Moyali says. She is beginning to speculate.

In the end, Moyali accepts Andrew and Waga on her list. In PNG cultures, people and alliances come above all else. She has little choice. At least the evil doctor is on hold.

The largest territory is not the Hunstein River watershed of Moyali's clan, but a vast area to the west, which includes flood plain forest as well as many of the foothills of the Hunstein Range. Its mascot is the Hornbill, and its leader, Ma Kenyafo, is a powerful, determined man, not easily swayed. He has already made up his mind as to what he wants to do with his property.

"All this flood plain swamp I'll keep for sago, gathering and hunting," he explains. "And this section here in the hills, where the two sandy creeks are, is where we like to vacation. We'll set that aside as a reserve for our own recreation, with our own rules." His handsome dark features glow in the dim evening light of Andrew's bark house. "Then all of this, from the bare face of the cliffs of Gelba, across the valley to the top of Mount Hunstein itself, can be a wildlife park. No plants and no animals are to be harmed there in any way."

Jay hires a helicopter for aerial photographs. I want to see the area from above so I go along. What we see is breathtaking. The rich variety of trees, vines and aerial plants form a massive entanglement of green scattered with red, white and yellow flowers. Black and white cockatoos and multi-colored parrots fly in flocks over the canopy. An eagle soars high above the hills below us. An astonishing white cliff rises hundreds of feet up out of the flood plain forest far to the north. Hunstein itself towers straight up above us into the clouds like some sort of giant green sleeping behemoth we must not disturb. The river sparkles and threads back and forth between the trees. Sunbeams light down through the clouds.

Jay and I make another trip over the area in the helicopter and this time we take Kenyafo along. His hands are locked in a death grip on the bar in front of him at first, but he beams with pride as we sail through the enchanting beauty of his realm. He recognizes it all.

"What do you think I should do, San Edie?" Moyali asks.

I think about how nice it would be if the swath which Kenyafo had proposed as a park extended further to include the beautiful realm we covered on the expedition; how important it is to preserve the Hunstein watershed; and how much the people depend on the land surrounding the village for food and supplies. I can only tell her I hope she won't lease any of her land for logging.

"But don't I *have* to lease the forest for logging at least on the foothills?" she asks, genuinely puzzled. "The forestry department said they wanted it, so I'll have to give it to them, won't I? We have to be nice." Just as she welcomed the outsiders, she feels she must allow logging companies in.

Once again I am frustrated. There is nothing more I can say. To protect the trees it seems the villagers like Moyali will have to change their entire ways of thinking. If only I could get closer to Bahinemos like her to better relate to them.

If I am not able to communicate on the level of clan ownership, how could I begin to explain to the villagers about the wiles of multinational companies? Perhaps I can at least counteract the myth from the forestry department which says they will be able to replant any trees which they cut down.

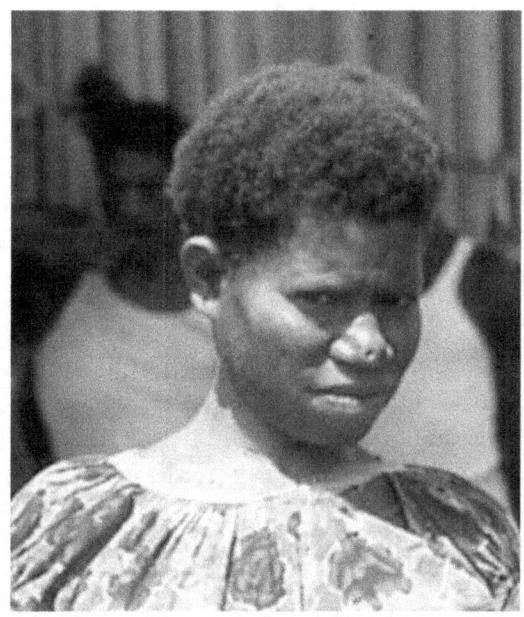

San Moyali

Cutting the pith from the sago palm to soak, drain, and eat

Chapter 7

A Task Unfinished

~~ At eighteen I was forced to face the terrible fate of having to move to the United States to get a Western education. Marriage, children and jobs kept me there, always against my will. ~~

It is time to go back to the U.S. I was disappointed at having spent so much time caught up in the clan registry, but everything had to be done one step at a time and that was the step the Bahinemos faced while I was with them. My dad went on to help them get the genealogies straightened out to every ones satisfaction. But they could still be changed. Anyway we were not at all sure whether fixing the genealogies had helped our cause or made it easier for the logging companies. I regret I can't stay to help with future challenges. The registry problems are only the first of many struggles which lie ahead as the Bahinemos make contracts, accept or reject logging proposals, and look for alternatives. I feel a desperate need to come back here.

I came wondering what would happen to the Hunstein Rainforest and the Bahinemos. I leave still not knowing.

In some ways the world depends upon the Bahinemos. The fate of a host of species of plants, and much rich wildlife which thrive nowhere else, is in their hands.

The scientific results of the expedition are astonishing: Mankind never before recorded at least 20% of all of the plant species the scientists found. PNG scientist Paul Katik, often referred to as the "walking dictionary" because he knows the names of more species of PNG plants than anyone else in the world, marvels, "In twenty years of collecting experience, I have never seen anything like this."

Wayne Takiuchi of the Bishop museum says, "This area is a botanist's gold mine. This is a totally different situation from the norm." In their six weeks, the scientists collected and processed about 1,500 different species in bloom, and this is not yet flower season. Mount Hunstein's geographic isolation explains this enormous volume of unique plants. The range also serves as a sanctuary for a tremendous variety of birds and many animals which are rare or exist nowhere else in the world except Papua New Guinea, including the new species of frogs.

In other ways the Bahinemos depend on the world: for information, for sources of income that will not destroy their forest or their lifestyle and for protection from money hungry companies.

As I fly out, I gaze out the window of the helicopter at a disappearing world. I am numb from leaving the forest and the people, unable to process the grief of this sudden departure.

We circle around, past towering lush vine covered trees, dotted with flowers and laden with bright screaming parrots. Will I see them again? Or are they just like frost on a window, beautiful and real to see and touch now-- but sure to vanish tomorrow?

When we reach the end of the barren lake, I look down. There is a patch of beautiful pink water lilies. The pads of the blue lilies are there, too. We fly down and circle them a few times, relishing the six-inch intensely fragrant blooms. The lilies are starting to return. The lake may once again come alive. I pray it will always be surrounded by magnificent, enchanting, virgin tropical rainforests.

Upon leaving Wagu, I must part with my family for a week and follow Jay to a coastal town called Madang to see the work of an active Japanese logging company. The magazine wants to show what could happen if they log the Hunstein. Rob and the kids take the week to visit the mission base where he and I met as teenagers.

On the way to Madang, Jay and I stay at Wewak where our family went snorkeling and we first met the scientists. This time I stay in the fancy hotel on the beach. But when I interview the Provincial Secretary, it is back in the home of some missionaries. Mr. Narokobi is the Provincial Secretary for the East Sepik Province. He is the man with the most power over the Hunstein area besides the Bahinemos themselves. He brings his wife and two children to the interview, and wears a bright casual cotton shirt with shorts. He is barefoot. We sit at the table so we can write notes.

"I, for one, don't like to cut any trees," he tells me. "Especially kauri pines. They are magnificent trees, straight up and perfectly round. Without intervention, loggers will completely wipe them out. But the province needs money. It's a question of economic gain for the province and the landowners. This is our frontier, and we *will* develop it."

"Maybe the Wagu villagers are happier the way they are, without development," I suggest cautiously. "Maybe they don't need development as long as they still have the forest to provide for them."

"They need money to pay for their education," he replies. "They need education. We can't leave part of the country behind. We'd have two castes--in the end that would lead to a separate elite."

"But, if we could get the same amount of money and local development from tourism," Mr. Narokobi says, "we would consider preserving all of the rainforest. Tourism would require expensive, well thought out development and a large investment to create lodges, airports and roads. We don't have the capital ourselves. But we do have non-governmental organizations like Wau Ecology Institute or the Foundation for East Sepik which could foster such an endeavor, if they could get a grant somewhere..."

As we talk, he grows more and more excited, postulating large international airports, plush hotels, scenic boat tours and hiking trails.

I think about the effects of such a massive bombardment of civilization and wonder who could manage it so as to allow the people to be guides, not gawked at. It all sounds like an unworkable dream to me.

We move on to Madang. Jay and I stay in one of those plush hotels Mr. Narokobi dreams of. The rooms are large and press right up to the calm ocean. I press a button by my bed and a curtain draws back on this vista. Another button brings forth cable TV. The dining hall presents exquisite cuisine and the music is live and rich. There are flowers everywhere and a free ranging pet hornbill. Large cages contain various other local animals. Waiters offer a constant array of elegant drinks as I wander the hotel gardens and dip in the pool.

This is the hotel from which the Melanesian Explorer, a small ship, makes its way up the Sepik river and brings tour boats to Wagu.

Jay and I opt for local tours. The hotel staff drops me off on a deserted island with another woman and together we picnic and snorkel with fish so plentiful and tame we can reach out and touch them. Their colors, patterns and shapes defy the imagination. The guides take Jay to a different island to scuba dive and he is equally impressed.

After the fun, we fly in a helicopter to the logging site. There is nothing there. Miles and miles of barren black dirt languishes in place of rainforest. No stump or leaf exists. I am stunned.

Around and around we go, trying to make a photo out of nothing. I get very sick in the helicopter and heave on everything. Consequently the pilot flies straight down into the middle of that vast expanse and drops me off for about twenty minutes. I am shocked and overwhelmed as I sit down on rich but thin black dirt which is already being washed away. Complete silence and desolation reign where once sang birds and pounded cassowaries. I think about the vast expanses of rainforest that once ruled the earth elsewhere and are now gone forever.

When they have finished taking photos, Jay and the pilot return to get me. In the evening I interview the German scientist who has been studying the area. Reimund Kube explains in simple terms what the best and the worst results of logging Papua New Guinea rainforests would be:

"A rainforest is irreplaceable. Once exploited, no matter how carefully, certain species will be lost forever. The large birds, cassowaries, hornbills, palm cockatoos and crowned pigeons will be the first to go. Gradually the other animals and plants will disappear as well.

"In a rainforest, unlike other types of forests, you can't fell large trees and expect new ones to take their place. One reason for this is all of the trees are tied together with vines, so one tree drags many others down with it as it falls. The resulting gap in the canopy creates far too much intense tropical sunlight for new little saplings to survive.

"If everything is done just right; if the foresters selectively leave the largest trees, build as few roads as possible and replant everything they take out, in thirty years you might get a sort of artificial forest. --That is *if* the soil is good and the ground is level to start with. Otherwise you would get a field of grass. The alternative, if the ground is good, is to go ahead and clear-cut a specific area, and then plant a sort of garden of the trees you want in its place. In as little as 15 years, you can harvest those trees, and thus avoid extending the area of damage. No one has ever yet been able to replace a damaged rainforest. No one knows if even 1,000 years would be long enough to accomplish such a task."

A rainforest will never grow back, I realize. Tangled jungle often reclaims abandoned sights but when a true rainforest is gone, it's gone.

<< >>

As far as my eyes can see there are bright lights, squared off cement roads and buildings. I am riding home from the airport with my family in a taxi in Dallas. Dallas is not known for smog, yet Sarah is holding her hand over her nose as the smell of petroleum in the city overwhelms us. If only I could have ignored the visa requirements and never boarded the plane out of PNG. A morose depression hits.

For months, it clings to me. I dream Moyali is tied to rafters and I wonder about the pressure she is under. I say many prayers for her and the forest.

Who can communicate with her? Can my article bridge the gap and show Westerners and villagers alike the intrinsic value of the rainforest? Will people with power read it? Will anyone do anything?

Will Moyali and the other Bahinemos succeed in saving their rainforest and culture like Angelina the soft furry baby phalanger we managed to bring to the United States with us? Or will life as they know it end in a short time like poor little Beasty who was mistaken for a rat and clubbed down before we left the village?

Despite my sadness, I write my article for *National Geographic*.

The magazine is thrilled with it, but there is a problem. While I write about the forest and the villagers, Jay's pictures are primarily of the people. The magazine wants both. Only pictures of the forest will bring it to the attention of those who might save it. After much deliberation, they decide they must have five more special rainforest pictures. Would I be willing to go back and take a different photographer with me?

Would I ever!

Chapter 8

Mt. Hagen: "We Shouldn't Be Doing This..."

~~ In High School while traveling through the highlands of Papua New Guinea I stopped at a roadside seller and bought an artifact. It appeared to be a hollowed out turtle shell and I wondered why it had nine notches in it. Curiously it fit nicely on my head. Too nicely! I finally figured out it was carved from someone's skull and the notches represented other kills. ~~

After a year back in the U.S., Rob and I return with a different photographer and without our children for a second expedition into the Hunstein Rainforest.

<< >>

As the nose of the jet angles down, I see scattered patches of coral looming toward me in the ocean below. The sea is turquoise under a smattering of white clouds. As I once again enter Papua New Guinea, anticipation engulfs me with joy.

This time *National Geographic Magazine* has commissioned me to lead my husband, Rob, American photographer, Max Schulbaum, and Papua New Guinea scientist, Karl Kerenga, deep into the Hunstein Rainforest. I return again to the place I love so much.

The article I wrote for them covered the culture of Wagu village; a scientific expedition highlighting the value of their forest; and the ominous logging proposal which hovers over the region.

To select our five required photos, our photographer will need to collect hundreds of photos from each type of forest on a trail up Mount Hunstein. This means several days of preparation and a two week trek in isolated rainforest. To save time we are stopping for supplies in Mount Hagen, hiring a helicopter to pick up carriers in Wagu, and flying directly into Gipa. From there we will hike to a cloud forest on the mountain. We will then hike out to Wagu and return by boat and plane.

The island of New Guinea is one of the least explored places on Earth. Western Europeans first contacted many of its people less than 100 years ago. The terrain is so wild and rugged that over 800 language groups exist in PNG on the eastern side of the island alone. Numerous plants, animals and birds are unique. Others are related to the most unusual flora and fauna of Australia. It is a land pregnant with mystery and adventure.

In one generation almost every individual in PNG has progressed from the Stone Age to the age of computers, airplanes and television. This development took the rest of us at least 6,000 years.

Though the Bahinemos have not yet come into the modern world, many Papua New Guineans have. In their own lives they have experienced the full range of human history, from the discovery of the wheel to animated cartoons, from appeasing the spirits of trees to plying the air with radar. Naturally, some find it all a little confusing, but on the whole they do a fantastic job of keeping up with the modern world. Their national system adapts to and competes with Western culture. Their feat is awesome. Yet, it is this ever encroaching civilization with its multinational oil, mineral and logging companies which threatens PNG's original cultures and their precious rainforests.

The smells of sweat and flowers, wood smoke and exhaust, ocean spray and fine road dust fill the air outside the terminal. Crowds of people mill about. Some yell. Some laugh out loud, and some even cry. Rob and I are at home with all this. Max, whom we learn has spent most of his career photographing luxury tours in other parts of the world, seems dismayed.

We had just met Max the day before when we boarded the same 747 in Los Angeles. Rob and I wonder whether he will be comfortable at the mission hostel where I have made reservations for the night. When I call to get directions, I learn that a large contingent of youth unexpectedly filled the hostel to overflowing. The caretakers offer to make room but I politely decline. We

summon a taxi and head for a standard luxury hotel where we take a
room on the 6th floor.

Our bed rocks violently back and forth, awakening us during
the night. Our first impulse is to blame each other, then, realizing it
is an earthquake, we bolt for the door. But there is no alarm and no
one else is evacuating. Are we too many stories up to make it down
to the exit before the shaking is over? The lower we envision going,
the more hotel mass we imagine frolicking above our heads.
Shrugging, we huddle back in bed. In the morning there is no
official news report. We hear from the front desk that it registered
seven on the Richter scale but no one seems concerned. When told
about our fright, local residents just laugh. We are in a different
world.

At noon the next day we soar over the southern part of the
island in a small DC-3 plane. As we head north toward the
highlands, we pass over an area which appears blank on all but
topographical maps. I try to see signs of the terrain which would
explain why no men of any race have ever penetrated this particular
area. There are rumors that no one who has attempted to explore
there has returned. I see nothing but green; miles and miles of
uncharted rainforest.

In a few days we will be immersed deep in uninhabited
forest --a rich world teeming with plants and birds and insects,
packed with surprises, and dripping with moisture.

Suddenly we make a steep climb into thunder heads as if we
want to ride their backs. Somewhere within them I know there are
mountains. We bump and jolt while rain thrashes at the windows.
Soon we are turning circles to get down, down, down through a tiny
hole to a green valley bedecked with a grass landing strip. Scraggly
porters unload our baggage in drizzling rain.

There are no taxis where we land in Mount Hagen so Rob
bargains with the owner of a van with a license to ferry people.

The approaching dusk, the rain and the complete absence of
official personnel or signs to direct us create an ominous first
impression of this town where we expect to meet our botanist and
spend four days buying and preparing supplies. This vague sense of

insecurity grows significantly as we approach our hotel, fortified with a ten foot stone wall and a massive gate surrounded by guards.

As soon as we arrive at the hotel, the staff informs us we have only forty-five minutes to buy the food and ingredients for the mixes which I need to prepare for the coming expedition. It is New Years Eve and the whole town is about to shut down until New Year's celebrations are over. No one can tell us when that will be.

"What kind of celebrations?" we wonder, as we hurry through the aisles of a small store. This is new behavior from when I lived near here as a teenager.

"Oh, they throw large rocks at cars and things like that," the store manager explains as he hurries to close early. He pulls a flare gun out of his pocket and leads us past a door guard holding a large club.

The hotel staff strongly advises us to stay off the streets for the next two days. Guards are everywhere. Is this what it is like when towns with tourist hotels replace small villages and rainforests?

The large hotel is empty, though a flier in the national newspaper advertises a New Year's bash to be held in the dining room that night. At six o'clock we head for the dining room and find we are the only three guests in a grand hall set for about 100. There are rows and rows of gourmet salads set out on a buffet along with exotic sea foods and a giant roast. As soon as we enter, white clad waiters appear from the kitchen and stand in a polite row. We select our food and sit at a table in a far corner with whistles, streamers, balloons and hats. Max promptly begins to tweet on his very loud whistle.

Our developing impression of Max is of a pleasant, jovial sort of person, ready to turn any awkward situation into a joke. Various sayings pepper his hearty New York accent. "As they say," we learn, means he is joking and "literally," means he is impressed. "That should be your biggest problem," is a cheerful antidote to just about anything. Max is a stout, middle-aged man who carries about him an air of success. Sparkling blue eyes light his face, touched with pink, and framed with graying hair.

It is almost time for the party to end, according to the flier, when about twenty other guests show up. For the most part, they appear to be old, white, colonial plantation managers, many of whom make it a habit to keep themselves surrounded by a contingent of local girls lured by a life-style they could never otherwise obtain. The girls hang on each other for moral support with frequent giggles as they endure the lewd gestures and passes that come with the arrangement. Soon streamers are flying everywhere.

At last, when the party is supposed to be over, a band shows up and begins to play.

There is plenty of alcohol and of course everything livens a little. The men seem to delight in throwing streamers and letting the air jet stream out of balloons like a group of goofy boys at a sleepover.

A tall thin man of about fifty seems to eye me constantly, so I am not surprised when he asks me to dance. As I try to keep pace with his long legs (I seldom dance), he whispers that he is from Britain and is the owner of the hotel. I am astonished when after many more gestures of invitation, and streamers and screaming balloons sent my way, he sits across from us and boldly informs me of his bedtime prowess and skills; meanwhile salting this description by informing Rob as to just how much money he has to offer, should the need arise. It's time for me and my husband to excuse ourselves.

A full moon lights the courtyard and crisp cool air creeps into our clothes. We are over a mile above sea level, we realize, as we find our way through shadowed gardens to our room. Inside we discover stacks of blankets line the room in lieu of central heat. I look out the window at a row of mountains edged with silver. All night long, off in the distance, revelers yell, beat on poles, pans and pots, and sing. Despite this ruckus, we feel safe and comfortable; cozy.

Tuesday, the guards continue to keep us encamped in the hotel for our safety. This is a taste of life in a part of Papua New Guinea that is culturally unbalanced due to the influences of civilization. The men set about repacking our load for the coming trek while I ask to use the kitchen to prepare granola and biscuit mix for the next four weeks. We weren't able to buy all of our supplies for the month in the forty-five minutes the day before, but I did gather enough to prepare the mixes we would need.

Although I am the only woman among us four, I am the official leader of the expedition because of my experience. My husband seems to have adapted to this well, and I am pleased. I have a lot of responsibility on my shoulders and I welcome his support.

I have estimated the amount of food we will need for four of us plus six carriers, based on experience from the much larger expedition the year before and numerous similar trips I made as a child. If my estimates fail, there will be no way to order more supplies. My goal for this expedition is to show our photographer how the forest looks at all the various levels of altitude. I have carefully calculated the minimum number of carriers I think we will need to get our gear up Mount Hunstein. The expedition will be without contact with the outside world for two entire weeks.

I ask around until I find the Papua New Guinean head cook, a stocky local citizen in bare feet and old clothes. He leads me to the hotel kitchen, which is large and ancient. Remembering the gourmet food, elegant tiered cakes and delicate decorated pastries of the night before, I am shocked to find the kitchen contains only a few rudimentary utensils and an old, enormous, stained and dented oven with just one heat setting. It is empty except for a few supplies in one lighted pantry. The contrast between the exotic, richly decorated food and that cellar of a kitchen leaves me stunned. I have five times as many ingredients and twice as much equipment in my U.S. kitchen, and would be hard pressed to come up with a simple pate.

A smartly dressed Englishman whom I haven't seen before solves part of this mystery when he passes by the entrance. The three PNG staff members who are in the room instantly drop everything and stand at attention, saluting and greeting him in strained English. He must be the force behind the show.

One of the cooks helps me find what I need, and together we measure my sixty cups of oatmeal, six jars of honey, and other ingredients. We chat in "Tok Pisin", the national trade language, and he tells me about the reign of unrest which has plagued his town in recent months. He attributes much of it to alcohol. He himself is suffering a hangover from the night before and has a black eye which he prefers not to discuss. I ask him what he plans to do in the afternoon and he replies, "Drink some more."

Although my eyes are brown and my hair is in a tight perm, I am pure Caucasian. However, some of the PNG hotel staff ask Rob whether I am a half-breed; a child of one of the plantation owners, perhaps. They simply can't believe a white woman could speak Tok Pisin with such fluency. In fact, wherever I go people often place me immediately in the right province by my accent and ask me if I came from a village there. Of course I let them know I grew up there, and that PNG is still home to me. Actually, I am quite pleased. I had been away for eleven years between high school and the previous year's expedition.

One fellow guest, stranded in the hotel with us, is an Australian gold miner in from the Western Province. After a minute of conversation I ascertain that his lifestyle is quite different from that of our historical American miners. He runs a large camp with massive equipment. "We get 3,000 grams of gold in every ton of ore," he tells me. "We cut into pure veins. PNG is the second largest gold producer in the world and is about to become the largest." He is on a four- day leave after working a month of seven-day weeks.

The conversation turns to the state of the country. More and more expatriates have been leaving Papua New Guinea because of an increase in thefts, assaults and even small riots in various towns. I wonder if this is the result of a poor system of crime prevention, or the sign of a nationwide cause of discontent. Poverty is almost non-existent in PNG. Education is available to all, and nationals run the government, so racial tension is not a significant issue. No one seems to be able to pinpoint any common cause for the country's turmoil.

The miner's answers are vague. He talks about landowners demanding payment for the land under his company's power line posts and even land crossed by the shadows of cables. "Then when you pay them, they don't know what to do with it," he says, "Sometimes we pay them thousands and it's all gone by morning." He also talks about how much more important relationships are to Papua New Guineans than money, and how a PNG medical doctor he knows, fully qualified in Australia, returned to his village and quit his practice entirely. "He lives off his own land, enjoys his wife and kids, and only on rare occasions intervenes in village emergencies," he says.

In all of our time in Mount Hagen the only white female residents I meet are a doctor and a pharmacist--whom I seek because of agonizing cramps on the third night in the hotel. The doctor diagnoses these as the side-effects of exposure to roach spray and advises me to change rooms. The manager, by this time quite embarrassed by his holiday behavior, seems very happy to comply with any request. Rob and I enjoy moving to a much nicer room free of charge while the manager allows us to spread out our things in the original room, which we use for repacking.

On the third day we are at last allowed to leave the hotel. Max is desperate to take some personal time to work on a travel book of his own, so I agree to let him take a private tour while Rob and I scour all of the shops in town looking for final ingredients to match our menu. This menu lists a recipe and an amount for every meal for us and the carriers for the entire two weeks we will be in the rainforest. We buy extras of everything, but we have to replace many items on our list with those less attractive to Western palates. No canned chicken for example, instead, steak and kidney pie.

Photo books about the highlands focus on the visible characteristics of the people. It is tempting just to sit on a street corner and stare at the crowd, but with the New Year's tensions still in the air, I think better of it. There are so many unbelievable sights: costumes, jewelry, women cradling pigs, chickens in bags fresh from the market. One old man converses in a bizarre combination of suit coat, shorts and bare feet. There are hats woven from colorful yarn and pieces of animal fur. Babies wearing only beads cling to parents' backs. Men and women in bright clothes with string bags, beads, safety pins, coins, birds' wings, paint and bark, parade the streets. I find every excuse to use the sidewalk from one store to another rather than take the car. Rob and I are enjoying our own tour.

By afternoon we have packed everything and realized that our helicopter charter the next day will never be able to transport our supplies. I had chartered the helicopter rather than a small plane so we could use it to shuttle the supplies and crew to Gipa, our base camp at the foot of the mountain. This would cut out two days of hiking. It would also allow me to avoid taking along extra carriers and their provisions. I planned to keep the expedition as small as possible. I wanted everyone to be treated as equals. I was bringing the same foods (not rice and mackerel) and tents for warmth for everyone.

A second helicopter on the site would be unnecessary and far more expensive to charter than a plane. However Wagu village, where we need to pick up our carriers, does not have an airport, so a plane would have to land at Ambunti, twenty miles down-river. From there a boat could transport our extra supplies to the village. Rob volunteers to accompany the luggage to Wagu himself by this route, so we decide to charter the plane. We make arrangements easily as air charter is still the primary form of transportation for many areas of PNG.

Rob was not raised in PNG as I was, but he knows the country, and also has a deep love for it. A Dutch citizen, his parents brought him to the mission field from Holland when he was a junior in high school. We met at the mission school, after which he followed me to the U.S. for college, where we settled, marrying and acquiring kids and jobs. Our previous expedition had been a dream-come-true for both of us. But now I find myself wondering if he is knowledgeable enough to direct an excursion of his own.

We have missionary friends who live at Ambunti and probably know where Rob can get a boat. He is confident enough in the trade language, and there are men in the area who know how to find Wagu. We decide he should set out early on the next day, like the rest of us so we can reunite in the village at noon.

On this last day of preparation for the expedition, botanist Karl Kerenga arrives from the coastal town of Lae. Karl has earned his reputation as a botanist and is second in charge of the Papua New Guinea Department of Forests. I expect a tall lowlands man, knowing he and his large family have a modern home in the coastal town of Lae. Instead he surprises me with his short muscular body, bushy beard and mischievous eyes. I soon learn that he comes from a Highland village not far from our hotel. Karl's English is excellent and he seems to be a quiet, quick and alert sort of person --or is it wary? He has been selected because of his position, so I know as little about him as I do Max, but I am determined to make us all a smooth functioning team.

After lunch the four of us find time to take in a short off-duty afternoon tour, compliments of Max. A PNG guide leads us to a traditional dance in a village of his own local tribe. In the highlands it rains almost every day, and we arrive at the village in the middle of a drizzle. While the rest of the group steps gingerly along the drier edge of the trail, I take off my shoes and luxuriate in the oozy mud my toes remember from the high school I attended in these same mountains. The forests have almost disappeared in the more populated valleys of the Highlands, replaced by grasslands centuries ago. Exotic species have gone. Somehow the people survived. However, recent complications due to civilization, such as alcohol and the breakdown of the family system, have had a devastating effect on their culture.

A fairly large gathering of villagers huddles in tiny round grass homes to keep rain from their costumes. In one hut I discover a very friendly group of women and children. Among them is a giant bird known for flying around at night with its large gaping mouth held open, hoping to run into bugs. A child is carrying two baby honey suckers, balancing in their nest with piteous cries. After a while the rain eases and the dancing begins. We take lots of pictures.

We are led to a point of land with mountains towering into clouds above and cliffs dropping into mists below. There, a hut introduced as the spirit house, is covered with feathered artifacts, clay pots and the bones of various animals. The people are warm and friendly and present a very ritualistic and fascinating performance of chants and dances.

The highlanders' brilliant feathered head-dresses tower three feet in the air and they have covered their bodies with paint, shells and intricately woven plants. I lean over and ask someone what the words they are singing mean. "They can't be translated into English" he hesitates. I ask again and he replies, somewhat chagrined, "The people are chanting, 'we shouldn't be doing this...We shouldn't be

doing this...We only do it for the tourists to make a lot of money...'"
They have repeated these same words the whole time! I suspect they
are dutifully keeping the spirits informed that the ceremony is just
an act.

By the end of the afternoon I am lost in a huddle of women
and children, enjoying their society even more than the magnificent
scenery, the intriguing ceremony, or the exotic costumes. Of the two
baby birds only one is left, which I feel quite sorry for and buy.

Chapter 9

Memories

~~ "Mommy, when am I going to get old enough to have dark skin like everybody else?" I asked, clutching my brown doll that I carried from house to house in the village in my little string bilum bag. ~~

The following morning, the baby honey sucker I adopted has rejuvenated under my care until it nearly swallows my finger each time I feed it. With careful feeding instructions, I pass it on to one of the cooks of the hotel. I hope the baby bird will be able to live on sterile food from the kitchen and will not become a meal in itself.

Rob left early in the morning by plane with most of the expedition supplies. Max, Karl and I have our last civilized breakfast and check out of the hotel. I forgot to ask for directions when I chartered the helicopter, assuming there would be only one available in that small town. There are, however, several companies of them used by gold miners, oil companies and the police, among others. By the time we find one with the name "Pacific Helicopters" on its side, we are quite late. The pilot grins at our apologies and says, "Your trip, your schedule." We figure by this time Rob should have already transported our supplies from the plane to the boat and be on the Sepik River. We expect he will reach Wagu village ahead of us.

The pilot directs me to the front seat with its glass bubble view in every direction, even down just beyond my feet. Security is only a seat belt, and I make mine snug. We put on ear phones and the pilot introduces us to the vehicle's intercom system through which we can shout short sentences above the deafening roar. Then, like one of those see-through elevators at a fancy mall, it goes straight up! In this case it gets faster and faster until we are way above the town and zooming forward. Yet, we are flying low enough to see cats on verandas and people hanging clothes on lines. Banana trees wave as we pass over, and so do some children. We wave back, but soon we are off beyond habitations. We follow a silver ribbon of river out of the green valley.

The island of New Guinea is shaped like a bird facing west, perched above Australia. A vast mountain range travels the entire length from its Indonesian head to its Papua New Guinea tail. Altitudes can be as high as 15,000 feet, as high as the Alps. So when we take off from Mt. Hagen at 5,300 feet, there are still higher mountains all around us. We head beyond this mountain cordillera toward the vast stretches of marsh and flood plain forest which make up the Sepik River valley. There, beyond where the main range of mountains meets the sea-level marshy plains, Mount Hunstein rises back up like a mist shrouded island to 5,000 feet.

Approximately 400 men, women and children own the 600 square miles of rainforest which make up the Hunstein Range. These are the Bahinemos. They divide themselves into four villages, the largest of which is Wagu. Vast areas of the Hunstein Rainforest remain completely unpenetrated even by them.

Our first expedition learned that mankind has never recorded nearly 20% of Mount Hunstein's plants. Unable to endure the flood plains to cross to other lofty mountains, many high elevation plants evolved their own types. Now their fate waits in human hands.

Although the Bahinemos adopted me at age four, I am neither a resident nor a PNG citizen so I can have no say in the decisions they are making. I want to educate them against the awesome pressures of multinational logging companies seeking profits and government agencies wanting development. Toward that end, on the first expedition I tried to understand the Bahinemo land owners and how they viewed the proposal in light of their own economic needs. I found it difficult to communicate to them the need to protect their land from loggers. Even my simplest suggestions toward saving it were difficult to get across. Civilization seemed to be getting the upper hand. Now I am bringing the Bahinemos' story to the world via *National Geographic Magazine* so that many will know about it and maybe provide more education and alternative economic resources. I, myself, hope to be able to get closer to the people on our expedition and thus be able to communicate better.

The river we follow tumbles out of the green valley and away to the east. The majesty of the land surpasses my wildest fantasies. We sail over verdant forested valleys, along tall cliffs and past magnificent waterfalls that take my breath away. Brightly colored parrots glitter in the trees below. First one eagle and then another soars high above the hills. The trees with their multitudes of shapes, colors and textures seem to be only a few feet below us as we cross a final ridge and descend toward the swamps.

Steamy tropical air fills our bubble cabin. We turn west and fly past an area of massive cliffs and falls that rises straight up from the heart of completely unexplored territory. Suddenly I am overwhelmed with the thought that the Hunstein area is only one part of a whole magnificent country, a country needing the world's support as the inevitable tide of humanity, driven to conquer and exploit for its own survival, laps against its pristine wilderness.

Moments later we follow a wide cut in the mountains. The pilot informs me this is the valley separating the Hunstein from the main range, and asks me to lead him to the village. I look to the north and recognize Mt. Hunstein itself. It looms straight above us into the clouds like some sort of beast sleeping peacefully. The Hunstein River weaves back and forth between the hills underneath us. I motion for the pilot to cross a low ridge. Wagu Lake spreads out before us like a vast, glistening, silver mirror. I point to the peninsula with the little village. As on the previous visit, the village swarms with people rushing to greet us.

So many memories flash through my head at once.

I look down at the place that had been my home off and on throughout my childhood whenever I wasn't away at the boarding school in the highlands. The villagers and I had watched each other grow up. When I returned on the first expedition the village was the same as I remembered it.

Most of the people, however, had changed. In their rugged environment they had become so much older than what I expected. In spite of that, on the first expedition I quickly renewed and deepened several relationships. Now I can't wait to be back with Ma

Jim and San Bahio, the young couple who were the cooks and the baby-sitters for my children, and Rob's and my closest friends. Their sense of humor, their zest for life and their young love brought richness into ours. I had missed them often during the past year.

As we zoom low in the helicopter, another person's face glides through my memory; the village elder who took care of me in the forest and is like a father to me, "Ma Lekim" or "Tied Vines." He stayed by my side throughout the entire expedition, telling me the stories of the ancestors, comforting me in times of stress, and often warning me of dangers only his experienced eyes could see. He still viewed everything in the context of the old ways, and it was he who taught me more than anyone how to see things through the Bahinemos' ancient cultural grid.

The Bahinemo pastor, Ma Gogomo, also comes to mind. I remember him most from the last expedition with a large happy smile and a glistening, muscular, bare chest. Hard working and enthusiastic, with a fathomless love for people and God, he was the one who carried my load up the mountain and talked to me for hours about what the Bahinemos knew of nature. He always asked how we Westerners thought things were, and then considered my answer pensively without showing any obligation to agree with me. If situations were hard, he poured three times as much effort into the solution than other men, huffing and grunting like a judo wrestler. If situations were impossible, he sang and prayed aloud until they passed.

My mind whirls with the thoughts of so many, many others who were not able to go with us on that first expedition, but whose lives had been deeply entwined with mine throughout my younger years. There were those with whom I played, or who had babysat me, and those I had carried in my own arms when they were babies.

One of those who had cared for me as a child was the red headed San Moyali, the widowed owner of all the land from the village to Mt. Hunstein. Her light skin and broad smile have followed me all of my life as she was my mother's best friend. Village politics seem to center around her.

In contrast to the highlanders, the Bahinemo people have a history of being primarily hunters and gatherers, not gardeners.

Disease kept their populations low, and surviving on the produce of the rainforest filled their lives. Unlike the Highlanders they are peace-loving and unpretentious in their worldview. Instead of elaborate costumes, they wear simple, cotton clothes to cover their dark slim bodies in the damp, tropical heat, much preferring them to traditional grass skirts. Their hair is universally cropped short and left unadorned.

I found it so hard to picture them while in the far away context of the United States, but now the details of their lives flood my mind as they themselves flood the edges of the grassy field onto which we are rapidly sinking.

When we open the cabin door, searing, sticky heat engulfs us. My dear friend Bahio is one of the first to arrive. She is panting, thoroughly out of breath. "The villagers expected you to land in the village square," she informs me, offering a warm embrace. Instead we had landed on the school playing field. Many more people run toward us. Very soon my elderly "uncle," Ma Lekim, runs up and grabs me in his arms. He squeezes me tight and blows air on both sides of my head, a precious and sacred show of affection.

Ma Lekim is still breathless as he announces that all of my worries about the forestry department are over. "The government representative says everything the scientists and you did was wonderfully successful." he blurts out with enthusiasm. "Now they can begin logging with new methods guaranteed to keep the forest intact. The signing begins next month!"

This is a complete misinterpretation of our desires and what we had said. How I wish it was possible for them to make money from logging and still save their forest. As yet, no scientist has come close to inventing a way to replant a tropical rainforest, let alone keep one intact while using it.

Ma Lekim and the other Bahinemos want desperately to keep all outsiders happy including government developers, scientists, friends and entrepreneurs. They value friendships more than anything else. The previous scientific expedition wanted to learn how great the value of the rainforest was before outside companies carelessly used it. Photographer Jay Dickman and I, along with *National Geographic*, wanted this documented. Now that we are all done, it is the developers' turn. The Bahinemos should please them next.

During the first expedition I learned the Bahinemos have no intention of living without their forest which still provides homes, recreation, favorite foods, traditional possessions and ultimately, their entire lifestyle. I spent many hours trying to explain the fact that logging would probably turn the Hunstein Forest into a grass wasteland. But as may happen again many more times in the future, the villagers had discarded all those elaborate explanations during my absence, with the arrival on the scene of new outsiders with their own opinions.

For several minutes I just stand and try to absorb all the faces gathered around me. Everything slows down and the barrage of noise fades into the distance as I orient myself to a dramatically different world. This is total immersion. Then I realize I am ignoring the pilot, Karl and Max. I return to the job at hand.

Crowds follow closely as we parade our way over a muddy path to the house my father built twenty-two years ago. After the last trip he donated it to the village church to use for visitors. Upon entering, we are surprised to find it functional. Although large holes render the screens useless, the basic structure seems intact. Water courses through the pipes to the faucets when they are turned on, though it is no doubt contaminated. The modern flush commode works. There are screens and bedding preserved in barrels. The bucket shower looks like Rob could repair it. We have a water filter in our luggage, in the load that should have come by plane and boat. But where *is* Rob?

Mount Hunstein over Lake Wagu

Ambunti on the Sepik River

Chapter 10

Money or Friendships

*~~ "Papua New Guineans will spend
money to gain friendships, while Americans
will lose friends in order to gain money."
Unknown PNG author ~~*

The dripping tropical heat is making us very thirsty and soon we will be hungry. The old stove is broken and of no use to boil the water. Nor is there a way to cool it for drinking. We are grateful when San Moyali volunteers to boil some water on her fire, and another friend offers to let us fix his kerosene burner to use as soon as Rob shows up with fuel. Meanwhile, Karl, Max, and I guzzle down three of the only six cokes we have brought for the trip. I am getting pretty worried about Rob but I must get on with my first task, choosing the carriers.

Months earlier I pre-selected a list of carriers whom I thought would work well together and provide the strength and talent we would need. I wrote to them in advance, informing them of our itinerary and asking them to gather on this day. Right away I note that the six persons I wrote to are present. I go over the plans with them again.

We must ferry the minimum amount of people needed for two weeks into the forest to the site called Gipa on the upper reaches of the Hunstein River. This will be our base camp. From there we will hike one day further and set up a second camp on the mountain's shoulder. From that camp, we will be able to reach high altitude forests for photos. We will address the flood plain forests at the base of the mountain at the end of our trip on the way back to Wagu, which we will come back through on foot. By then supplies will be lower and loads lighter.

"Is the river level low enough to allow the helicopter to land at Gipa?" I ask. Several people report that the water is low enough to expose sandbars but the brush has overgrown the sandbar nearest to Gipa, so we will have to land further downriver. If we do that, our load will have to be hand carried back upriver in shifts, as we are flying in many more supplies for base camp than our carriers can carry on their backs. This will waste an entire workday.

Finally, one Wagu man suggests that the helicopter shuttle in four teenage boys right away to the place nearest to Gipa where they can land. The boys would spend the night there, hike to Gipa in the morning and clear a closer sand-bar with machetes. They could come back to Wagu the next day on the return of the first helicopter shuttle. I tell the pilot this plan and assure him that one of the boys speaks English. Immediately they are off. In six minutes the pilot returns alone. "It won't be a problem," he says. "We landed right at Gipa but it will help to have them clear a little more room."

Right then the distant hum of Rob's motor canoe sends up a cheer of relief. It sounds like a bee and the hum increases slowly for several minutes until the boat becomes visible as a dot at the far end of the lake. As Rob reaches the shore, I see that the noon sun has broiled him like shrimp. "I didn't have the sunburn lotion with me," he exclaims. Perhaps the absence of convenience stores is the greatest difference between our Western idea of wilderness and the *real* frontier. Rob is tall and tan with brown eyes and black hair, but his skin is not ready for hours of equatorial sun. It looks like Rob will spend several miserable days and nights waiting for his skin to peel. I was right to be worried about him.

"A helper dropped our drums of helicopter fuel into the first canoe we rented," Rob explains in reference to his lateness, "and it broke through the bottom. It took all morning to make amends with the owner and hunt down another boat." In the end, the only boat he found strong enough to hold the fifty-five gallon drums our pilot needed for his return flight was another canoe, this time an old fashioned dug-out carved from a log. Each time the canoe turned, the fuel sloshed outward against the curve, tipping the boat so that Rob was sure they would capsize. As the channel to Wagu village is full of hair-pin turns every hundred yards, Rob's nerves are almost as raw as his skin.

These problems seem somewhat routine, however, compared with the serious matter which begins to engulf me. *National Geographic* chose me to lead this expedition for one special reason above all else, my rapport with the carriers. Several times during the first expedition, the carriers almost mutinied. On the most recent botanical expedition, the carriers threatened the leader with physical attack. Karl had attempted to make an expedition on his own and had backed out because of the weather. But, he confessed to me in private that he was in fact afraid of carrier problems.

I believe the Bahinemos compete well with the average Westerner in pride, temperament, kindness, intelligence and dedication to work. Indeed, cultural differences caused all of the problems on the first expedition. I am confident we can avoid trouble on this expedition with careful communication and the right carriers. I had selected carriers I know and with whom I work well. Complications begin at once.

In the process of selecting my carriers back in the U.S., I interviewed Wayne Takeuchi, a scientist in Hawaii and the leader of our previous expedition. Of all outsiders, I knew Wayne was the leader the village appreciated most, in spite of an occasional threat against him.

"One Bahinemo gave me a list of the very best workers," Wayne informed me, "and many of them were women." These reportedly could carry the most weight and had caused no trouble except that their husbands grew resentful when the women received more pay than the men. He couldn't remember who the trusted man was who had given him this list, but suggested Ma Wamseli. Wamseli is known to be rather independent, but he was a great help to Jay as a photographer's assistant on our previous expedition. He had also worked for my parents many times when he was a boy, so I found this quite plausible. Wayne promised to mail me the list when he found it.

I received a list of six adult women and a few teenagers. Included among the women were the wives of Wamseli, Jim, my good friend and guide from the year before, and Gogomo, the hard working pastor. I chose those three couples and determined to pay each person the same amount. The three couples I selected had been my friends all my life and I had no doubt that I could trust them to support and protect us. When I wrote the letter asking them to be ready, I added my mother's friend, Moyali, as a stand in, in case any of the others couldn't make it. Everything seemed quite simple.

After a couple of hours in Wagu, however, the pastor informs me his wife is unable to find a baby-sitter for their many children and therefore can't go along. Ma Gogomo is the strongest, most honest, responsible, hard worker known. We need him. He agrees to travel alone and I set about to find someone to replace his wife.

The villagers are appalled when I ask for San Moyali, our back up person. How terrible for Gogomo to take a single widow in place of his wife, they say. I understand why they see it that way and begin asking about other possibilities.

I then learn that Ma Lekim has been hurt because I did not list him. As my closest adopted relative and the most mature older person, all the Bahinemos agree that I should have selected him first. He assumes I made a mistake and is most eager to replace Gogomo's wife. I value my relationship with him and don't want to damage my deepest connection with the village, especially with its history. The more I think about it, the more I realize that to leave him out would be an unpardonable cultural offense.

It is at this point that my mind begins to switch back and forth between American thinking and Bahinemo thinking. To facilitate a smooth functioning team of both Europeans and Bahinemos, I will have to understand their opposing world views and be able to make compromises between them. In this case, however, the two sets of logic lead to opposite choices. Both views make perfect sense by themselves but have no common ground on which to work out a compromise. I am to compare apples to oranges and select the best. Most people would simply follow the logic closest to their inherited world view, whether Western or Papua New Guinean. In time, faced with many such situations in a given circumstance, one could learn which culture is more important to follow in each event. I need to make immediate decisions pleasing to both.

Most Papua New Guineans believe relationships are more important than money. Bahinemos aim for friendships and expect to earn some money in the process. Westerners base their decisions around profit and expect to cultivate some friends in the process.

While friendly, *National Geographic Magazine*, an American organization, values money. They hired me to collect pictures as economically as possible, not to maintain friendships. The reason I had left my elderly "uncle" off the list was because he was too old to carry more than thirty pounds. Other carriers could carry twice as much.

Max, Karl and Rob beg me to "just say no" to his request to join us. They think I am being too soft by considering him for the job, and that mixing business with friendships is always a disaster. When I continue to hesitate, they become exasperated. Don't I realize we have already brought way too much luggage for six strong carriers?

When I try to explain all this to Ma Lekim it upsets him more. He is as strong as ever, he insists, and will try twice as hard out of his love for me. He appreciates my concern for his health, but have I thought about the wisdom which comes with age? "Do young men know the real forest secrets?" he asks. I know they do not. For a moment I feel panicked with confusion.

I select Ma Lekim.

Another complication regarding the carrier list arises. Ma Wamseli and his wife, San Yamu, have no one to care for their nine year old son. They won't consider leaving him with a baby-sitter. They insist he could help with chores and carry his own food. I look at the boy and see that he could eat as much as an adult and take up a full seat in the helicopter. What am I to do? I want Wamseli because I feel I know him well, and Yamu, though much older, is both strong and reliable. We must include the boy.

To my relief, Ma Jim and San Bahio present no complications.

It's time for the carriers to try on their loads and to add up our weight for the helicopter. The pilot informs me the cost of our charter to the village is twice as much as a previous employee estimated for me. In addition, with the airplane and boat charters we added, we more than strained our allotted air transport funds. The extra shuttle to clear the sandbar was the last straw. There is no way we can afford more than two shuttles to base camp. However, as everyone gathers the luggage it becomes obvious there is way too much. We need at least two more carriers!

I return to Moyali, the widowed friend of my mother, whom I have just turned down and ask if there is someone with whom she can travel. She recommends her teenage son. They are both already packed, she says. She hoped I would allow him to come as a chaperone so she could replace the pastor's wife. I don't know much about Moyali's son, who uses the Western name Mathew, except he will one day be the land owner in her place, and that he seems a little spoiled. Villagers tend to butter up to him, knowing if she died, he would be in control of all the land they use for resources. Maybe I need to get to know him better, too!

This makes nine carriers. I brought food and shelter for six. I provided some extra supplies for contingencies, but would they be enough for three extra people? After much discussion with the villagers, I decide to rely more heavily than planned on fish from the river, wild fruits and herbs and dry chewy sago cakes, made of the starch of the sago palm. Someone finds some extra tarpaulins from the previous expedition. I keep the details of these solutions from Rob and Max for now. I figure they will handle them more easily when hungry.

We finish dividing the supplies, and the carriers try the loads on again. There is still far more equipment and food than they can carry. I wonder how I could have been so wrong in estimating our weight allowance until I realize Max has brought with him at least twice as many heavy suitcases and bags for cameras as the photographer from the previous expedition, whom I had used for my calculations. All together, five steel suitcases of cameras, lenses and film, plus several bags of personal gear, belong solely to him.

Now what am I supposed to do? Briefly, I consider sending in a whole separate contingent of carriers on foot, but they would each want to be fed. I planned to treat everyone as equals on this trip, meaning European menus to go around and tents for each couple. It is too late to consider a completely different kind of expedition, bringing along half the village and feeding them rice and fish. We might have to dump some of our cargo. Rob and I decide to carry loads ourselves. This makes us one with the carriers. Karl also agrees to carry a pack. He is in good shape and can at least carry his own things. We hold our breath while the pilot calculates the weight one more time. "Two trips," he announces. We are on.

Rob, Karl, Max and I are exhausted. Dusk descends fast, so we send the carriers home to rest for the night.

Over rice, fresh beef and stir-fried market vegetables, Karl and Max continue to express consternation over my selection of carriers. "What does it matter what the villagers think!" they exclaim with exasperation. "Why not pick the eight strongest young men in the village?"

About the time I am running out of ways to convey my emphasis on relationships as the secret to getting Bahinemo carriers to work without incident, Karl remembers he has a copy of Wayne's complete original list with him in his backpack. Wayne found it at the last minute and sent it to Karl, thinking it might be more likely to reach Karl than me. It lists six married women and six single young men. "Under no condition should you take Wamseli" it reads, "and stay away from Solomon [my "Uncle Lekim"] as he is much too old and cannot carry enough to make it worth your money."

It's time for bed. While the two single men use their tents to protect them from malarial mosquitoes, I hunt down a large, old double net from a storage barrel which is mercifully cooler on Rob's sunburn than the tents. Pink blisters cover most of his body.

As I lay in bed thinking of the new men and women on our team, I am glad I have chosen friends and key leaders rather than strong young backs. Hopefully this trip will give me a chance to learn to really understand the Bahinemos and be able to bridge our cultures and perhaps communicate the need to save the rainforest.

Besides, imagining those recommended married women on Wayne's final list alone in the rainforest with those young men, is enough to make me shudder. I decide it is a good thing I didn't find the list in time.

L-R: San Edie (author), San Bahio, Ma Jim, Ma Wamseli, Ma Rob

Solomon or 'Ma Lekim' to Edie

Chapter 11

Which Way to the Mountain?

~~ It was always a challenge to get off of the muddy bug-filled ground. When I was a teenager my Dad tried to make a platform for our family out of three inch branches. He built a frame two feet up off the ground and then laid a series of branches horizontally across it, two feet apart. He covered the whole contraption with a tarp, expecting each person to sleep on the tarp in the spaces between the branches. It was a hilarious disaster. Whenever one person got up, without his weight to keep things balanced, the tarp in the spaces next to him instantly sagged down, dropping people to the ground. We bobbed up and down all night. ~~

It's noon the next day when the carriers have the gear assembled under the guava trees down by the helicopter.

None of us visitors slept well during the night with the noises of the village clamoring through the old screen house. Personally, I welcomed the atmosphere for the memories of my childhood it brought back. For the other non-villagers the night was "literally" (to quote Max), an awakening after the cozy hotel. Dogs howled, babies cried and families quarreled, sounding as if they were right in our rooms. As the night wore on these noises were replaced with the sounds of exotic frogs, insects and owls, and worst of all with the eerie screams and flaps of giant flying foxes. Just before dawn roosters took up their shift and began to crow, one of them right outside the window. In the morning, the village crowds returned early with numerous issues for me to address during my short visit.

The crowds of villagers move to the helicopter and gather in curious clusters around the final thirteen expedition members for a grand farewell.

The Bahinemo women on our team wring their hands in terror about the helicopter ride. They keep talking and talking about it, trying to psych themselves up as we would for some new thundering thrill at an amusement park.

Each team member is about to become "rich." With employment opportunities non-existent, the standard amount I pay should provide each of them with approximately a year's average salary at the end of two weeks. If we had given this advantage to teenagers, as the note from Wayne directed, it might have upset the whole community. I look forward to spending time with mature, sensible people I can trust and get to know in a serious way.

Our pilot loads the helicopter to its absolute maximum capacity with four people across the back seat and one in front. Then he fills all of the cargo holds and even the outside baskets full of luggage. They hold quite a bit less than half of what we have with us. The first shuttle leaves and returns in a few minutes to re-load five more people and half of the bags and boxes left waiting on the pile. Karl, Max and I will have to take a third shuttle. This will not fit our budget.

As we soar over the ridges that surround the great mountain, we notice for once it is free of clouds. Max and I request some aerial shots. "But it's all on my time," the pilot protests. This last trip wasn't predicted by the pilot's calculations and he isn't charging. We are too close to the mountain to get perspective, anyway. It just looks like a great big hump.

"Take her down," I say, and around we swirl. It's the last time we will get a clear view of the mountain.

The long, straight limbs of the tall kauri pines, the trees most prized by loggers, poke above the thick, green canopy under us like clusters of fuzzy sticks. We descend steadily all the way to the foot of the mountain. Then we slip down between the trees to a small, rocky sandbar. The four men who have spent the night clearing the sandbar are waiting for a ride back to the village. Above the roar and cyclone of the helicopter blades they frantically try to tell me something. With every minute burning expensive fuel, the pilot is already buckling them in when I finally understand their message. "He landed at the wrong place!" they yell. "We spent all day clearing Gipa, and this is not Gipa!"

"It's just up the river," the pilot points. I turn to the young men again. They are still alarmed.

"We'll pay you anyway!" I yell above the din. They smile. Then they are gone.

Deafening silence settles around us as though the lid of the forest has slammed shut. All ties to civilization have been obliterated in seconds. Clearly the two cannot mix. The river babbles a few feet away and harmless bees hum through delicate white flowers at my feet. All around us trees of every imaginable shape and size, piled high with vines, blockade the forest from the river. A soft breeze blows down off the mountain, and it's cooler than it was in the village. Soon the cicadas begin their distant drone. Odd bits of luggage from the other shuttles are scattered around the sand bar. No one from the previous shuttle is in sight. We three stand on the rocks alone. Does anyone know where we are?

Rob appears from the forest where he has waited since the first shuttle. "It's a terrible mistake," he tells me. "Ma Lekim tried to tell me while we were still in the air but I didn't understand him. He was the only one who recognized this was the wrong spot. I guess the boys didn't realize it yesterday when they told the pilot where to land. Anyway, the carriers say it's not too far, and they're willing to make several trips to get all of our cargo transported."

Some luxury items to be enjoyed only at Gipa, our base camp, such as fresh vegetables and extra utensils are packed loosely in boxes and bags. Each person will have to make at least two trips to get all the supplies from the sand bar to camp. Rob and I both grab packs assuming the carriers couldn't have gone out of earshot. But Karl and Max are awestricken by the blue, purple and yellow butterflies hovering over several different kinds of flowers and set about immediately to photograph some. "Why not camp here," I wonder, eyeing the river, the sandbar and the mountain towering gloriously above. But the carriers, having vanished, cannot be asked to make camp.

At first Rob and I try to follow their trail. "It is only a short ways," they told Rob. But we lose their tracks when we get to the river. On our side of the river there is only thick jungle with no sign of penetration. The water in the river itself is deep. Confused, we lay down our loads. The sun beats sharply, and Rob, still raw from the day before, works his way to the only point of rocks harboring shade. I slip into the cold, clear rapids, then cut into the forest alone in the direction I believe the trail should be. I find nothing.

We wait. There isn't a doubt in my mind that the carriers will return. Nor am I afraid. I have loved this river since as early as I can remember. Blue swallows flicker and play back and forth. Somewhere in the distance a parrot calls out. It's a beautiful afternoon.

Karl and Max, however, while still taking pictures of flowers on the rocks and sand, are not so sure. Carrier mutiny is one of the greatest fears of Westerners in a rainforest, and being abandoned so soon seems to them an ominous sign. It only deepens their suspicions regarding my choice of the carriers.

An hour passes. The sun drifts slowly across the sky, and Rob moves to new rocks in order to stay in the shade. Cicadas continue their monotonous drone in the trees around us, partially drowning out the gurgling river.

At last, several brown faces emerge from the forest. The carriers laugh when they see where Rob and I are waiting at the end of the tracks I followed. "We thought you knew where the trail was, San Edie. You've been here before. Why did you head up the river when the trail goes inland?"

I show them the tracks I followed and they are puzzled. Then one remembers. "Those are from Ma Wamseli and his son, who followed the river a ways to scout fishing holes."

The last pieces of cargo are gathered up and we duck under trees and vines to the real trail. Camp is a forty-five minute hike away. From the air, it might have looked like a ten minute walk. We are now two days hike from Wagu; a flight of five minutes.

A waist-high patch of bug infested grass envelopes me. There is a sick tightening in my throat as I realize this is Gipa, the camp I remember from the year before as a deeply shaded glen of

clear forest floor which looked out onto a rock bar and then the
river. Perhaps thirty trees have been cut, allowing thick grass and
weeds to grow, spoiling the view as well as the atmosphere and
harboring a host of alarming insects. The camp is now hot and sticky
as we pick our way through the ruins of the old bunkers which are
nothing more than piles of rotting sticks.

"Who cut the trees?" I ask, stifling my rage.

"The botanists", Karl admits sheepishly, "after you left at the
end of the last expedition. They were afraid of branches falling on
their heads." I am devastated but must make the best of things.

Everyone sets about to build new structures for tarps. This
means cutting and hauling saplings and tying them into a framework
with vines. Rob, Max and I opt to have our tent frames set up away
from the river in the rainforest where the old shady conditions exist
even without a nice view. This separates the camp along racial lines
which doesn't make me happy, but it is truly only a difference in
taste. We prefer the unknown risks of the forest over the known
discomforts of heat and bugs. They would rather face the bugs to be
near the river and out from under precarious trees.

Ma Lekim looks alarmed when I show him the places I have
in mind for us, even though I point out that the branches above them
seem sturdy. He frowns and says nothing, but begins to pace the
area, looking down at the ground.

"You can build your shelters here and here," he says sternly,
pointing to two mushy, humpy places which are much too close
together. I start to protest but notice the serious concern in his eyes,
so I tell the men building our tent frames to comply with his
instructions. Some bark is salvaged from the old camp beds for
above ground platforms so we won't feel the humps and mud. Max
is grateful for the platform and doesn't seem to mind being so close
to us, so I don't have to explain anything.

It rains almost every night of the year in this rainforest. Dark
clouds soon begin to gather. When the sapling frames are secure, we
cover them with blue, nylon tarpaulins. The Bahinemos build one
long shelter using the tarps they brought from the village. The
couples put their tents under these tarps. The other carriers lay their
bedding between the tents. Everyone tries their best to guess where

water will gather into great reservoirs and burst through the tarps, or simply breeze in through the sides.

In addition to the tents, I have brought along three screened jungle hammocks. Max chooses one to use as a tent under his frame and tarp. The other two are happily claimed by Karl and Gogomo who decide to hang them in the traditional manner from trees rather than to harvest more materials in order to build platforms for themselves. I think they are glad to be out from under the same shelter as all those women.

Jungle hammocks are difficult to find now that the Vietnam War is over. No one who used them then seems eager to pass the experience on, though they are wonderful for the environment. Made of heavy military nylon, surrounded by screen, and covered with a light nylon roof, they make quite a contraption. One's first task is to try to hang them right side up while the weight of the roof keeps pulling them upside down. Once the main hammock strings have been tied tight between two good trees, the roof strings must be tied equally tight a few inches above them. The roof must then be spread flat with sticks wedged from side to side. Unless everything is done to perfection, water runs down the strings onto the sleeper when it rains.

Setting the hammocks up, however, is only half of the battle. To get into one, instead of just sitting sideways in the middle and turning to a sleeping position, one must squeeze in through Velcro doors while keeping bugs at bay. As Karl and Gogomo demonstrate, the first few attempts leave most users with a new and intimate understanding of the ground.

One of the women heats water over a hot fire. A combination of rice, soup, canned meat and dried vegetables makes a quick, hearty meal and everyone relaxes.

Darkness hits fast on the Equator. When chores are finished and all equipment is tucked under the tarps, some of us take turns heading for the cold river to wash. No one wears bathing suits so "danger" is the view for those looking your direction when lightning flashes.

Before long, Rob and I crawl into our sleeping bags and wonder at the pitch darkness of the tropical rainforest night. With the flashlight off we cannot see our hands in front of us. It is a trick not to bump each other in startling, unpleasant ways, i.e. "Please get your elbow out of my nose!" Just as we get comfortable, heavy drops begin to fall. Seconds later their patter grows to a pounding roar. We hold each other tight as large leaves and twigs pelt our tarp. Distant thunder adds to the strange, exotic lullaby.

The storm saturates the camp but the sun is right on time. We pass out coffee and bowls of hot oatmeal and string up lines to dry our wet things. Max and Karl go right to work collecting flowers while the rest of us improve the camp, including building a cook house where we can stand if it rains during the day.

Early in the afternoon, Rob and I set out up the river to explore. It is Sunday, and I feel bad that we are not holding a service as the carriers expect, but not everyone is of the same religion. I don't want to offend anyone or make anyone feel proselytized under my leadership. Instead I let everyone have the day off. They are free to do as they please as soon as the camp is set up. Rob and I can't wait to explore and swim in places along the river which we cherished the year before.

We are not disappointed. The river flows crystal clear around rock bars, under logs and through deep pools. It is cool, but not cold, and we sink into it with pleasure. The sun dances on moss covered cliffs dotted with tiny flowers. What has always lured me most about the Hunstein River is its purity; no footprints except those of wild things, no litter and no trampled grass. There are so many treasures: beautiful stones, driftwood and exotic seeds lying where they fell. A little bright blue kingfisher darts away from a high dirt bank. Now and then some wild cockatoos scream in the distance. Fruit doves coo one gentle song while wild mynas seem to speak in tongues. Orange colored blossoms hang down from vines far above, and butterflies hover in colorful clusters wherever there is wet sand.

A few bends up the river, we come across the waxy fruit I often gathered as a child. I collect a few, savoring their rich, tart flavor, and decide to cut across alone through thick forest to an old river bed where I know Max and Karl are supposed to be. Perhaps Karl can identify them. Rob doesn't mind waiting by the river, as he is still not used to being off trails. I am careful to duck under and aside small branches since I have no machete and such branches are often the bearers of wet leaves, which can harbor hornets, leeches or other unpleasant surprises.

I find Karl and Max after about ten minutes just as Max is returning to camp. He had asked Mathew, Moyali's son, to refill his canteen, which the boy had promptly done -- from the clear but un-sterilized river. This partly explains the pallid look on Max's face. I go back into the forest, this time scouting for a clearer way to bring Rob. Together we both follow Max. Sweat pours down Max's face and he is panting in loud hisses with exhaustion. Karl walks beside us and confides that he doesn't think Max will be able to make it on any "big" hikes. He suggests Max stay in camp after lunch while he and some others go out to hunt for flowers to bring back. I urge Max to replenish his electrolytes and rest. I suspect he might be more dehydrated than tired, but he admits that he doubts he will get far in this environment. I try to hide my dismay, but conclude that I should wait and see if he adjusts to the surroundings before taking any action. We can't stay here long. We must go on to higher places.

In the evening San Moyali, the widow, and San Bahio, the young friend who helped me cook before, help me put together "Hobo Stew", an American camp dish where potatoes, meat and vegetables are placed in foil and baked. With the extra amount of people to feed, it takes much longer than we expect to get all the foil packages done on the coals and ready to eat.

In addition, some of the potatoes have been mislaid in the dark, meaning each person only gets one. We are also short of canned meat. Wamseli brought back a fish to add to the meal, but he lays it whole across hot coals, face and all, so I do not think the non-Bahinemo travelers will be able to stomach it. I put more meat in the Westerners' packets. This is the second time treating the Bahinemos and the Westerners equally, has proven difficult. Thankfully the Bahinemos don't resent getting less tinned meat. The meal is scant, and by the time the food is ready the sky is very dark. I think about making up some of the biscuit mix, but Karl and Max are as exhausted as they are ravenous, and Rob's sunburn is raging, so they go straight to bed.

I stay up with the carriers around the campfire after everything is put away for the night. I plan to spend as much time with them as possible in this way. I hope that our nightly conversations will enable me to convey the true worth and fragility of the trees around us.

I also worry about Max making it up the mountain. So do the carriers.

"Max only went a few feet before he stopped, huffing and panting," Jim says. "We don't see how he will ever make it up that big ridge, even by a different route."

With this comment, the conversation turns to the various attempts to find Mount Hunstein. "The first route, the one they called `20 Mile', even though it was actually much less, was terrible!" Ma Jim exclaims, his young, handsome dark features standing out in the dim light. Others nod in agreement.

"That was the route that you went up last time," several inform me.

"It was not even in the right direction, and going up it was like climbing trees." says Gogomo.

I do remember the route as being steep, and that we never came near Mount Hunstein's summit. Because I didn't have to haul a pack, I hadn't realized what an issue this was for my two carriers.

"There is a new route which Wayne's recent expedition navigated, and it is much easier. It takes longer though, and it also goes up the wrong ridge," explains Gogomo further. The others echo this information.

I sit silently, contemplating my mission to get Max up at least to cloud forest. It is difficult to tell whether he really is unfit he just needs to get acclimated. This entire expedition is for the sole purpose of getting pictures of each type of forest. Forests on the lower river could have been reached by hiking in from Wagu, and wouldn't have required an expensive helicopter.

I have a radical idea. All of us believe that the scientists took the wrong route up Mount Hunstein on the first National Geographic Expedition. Consequently, only two of them could even claim to have reached the top. That would have been at the end of an exhausting two-days-in-one hike from the very farthest camp, which we had no plans to reach. Time and again I have stared at the topographical map wondering why they took the wrong route. The map shows a gentle slope, straight toward the mountain. It looks about two days shorter

We have one more day planned in Gipa. What if a couple of guys and I check out the route that seems the most sensible on the map? We wouldn't be wasting any time looking while Max takes photographs, and just maybe, it might turn out to be much easier for everyone.

I tell the carriers my idea. Then I strain my eyes into the flickering dark to search for their reactions. "Of course, I think it's a wonderful idea," Ma Wamseli says. But I want to hear from someone with more authority.

"Do you think it's wise to change plans this late, San Edie?" Ma Gogomo asks. Gogomo is expressing my own doubts. But my father taught me how to follow a topographical map in a rainforest years ago, so I know much more about the route than he could guess from mere speculation.

"What about you, Ma Lekim? What do you think?" I ask.

Ma Lekim has been listening in silence. It appears to me as though he is deep in thought. Elders never speak until the rest are through; until they have considered everything. When they do speak, it's conclusive.

"What does this map of yours say about this route?" he asks. "Tell me everything you know."

I retrieve the map and describe the route, specifying rivers to be crossed, ridges to be paralleled and the apparent terrain. From time to time he asks such detailed questions as, "And at that point, what is off to your distant left?" He appears to be following every word intently.

Suddenly, he sits straight up and clears his throat. "Ahem. This is the right way." he announces. "This is the way of our ancestors. This is the way my father took me when I was a child. Edie is telling the right way to the mountain!" He is elated. Then he stops with a quizzical look on his face and asks me, "Why didn't the first white men that came to scout out the trail follow this map if it says all this? Why did they go to the wrong ridge? I tried so hard to tell them they were wrong, but they would not listen to me. I am an old man. They only listened to young people."

"It's true, San Edie," the others say with unease. "They didn't even take Solomon (Ma Lekim's real name) along, and the rest of us didn't know the right way. They just looked at the horizon and said, 'Take us up there!' So we took them up. They didn't consult a map, and none of us had any idea what they wanted."

"When we found out that they wanted us to haul all their cargo up that steep ridge to see a mountain that wasn't even really there, we were furious." Wamseli explains, "We thought of chopping them up with knives," he yells (shedding light on the note which warned us against taking him.)

Seeing the alarmed look on my face, all of them laugh, breaking the tension, "It's just a saying, San Edie; we would never do such a thing, really. But we were mad."

I do not know what the Western side of the story is, other than that the scientists accomplished their goal of studying high altitude flora and fauna. I don't know what they would have to say about why they headed south instead of southwest, so I can add nothing.

Ma Lekim begins to describe what he remembers about the route I have just proposed. His slim wrinkled figure leans in toward the fire causing flickers of light to reflect on his bald head. "You are right about this route, San Edie," he says, "how it crosses two rivers and then crosses the main river just after its fork. From there you begin to climb slowly, not steeply, and it continues all the way to the cold places. We never went past the cold places. None of our ancestors ever went into the cold lands. They thought there were too many spirits there. But there is a lake just before you get to them, in the middle of the ridge."

"A lake!" I exclaim. "But there's no room for a lake. It would have to be on my map if there was one."

Lekim looks quite disappointed, "There surely is a lake," he says. "Our ancestors camped there and ate sago from the palms on its shores. I do not know about your map. It cannot show every tree. It shows much wisdom, but perhaps it does not know about the lake."

I can't disagree with him out loud. He is an elder. But I seriously doubt that there could be a lake. The map shows steep drops on either side of the ridge.

It's late, and one by one people around the fire begin to fall asleep. As they do, their spouses or friends rouse them and send them into their tents. I, too, am ready to join Rob in mine, so I excuse myself, but suggest that they consider whether any would like to escort me to search for a completely new trail the next day.

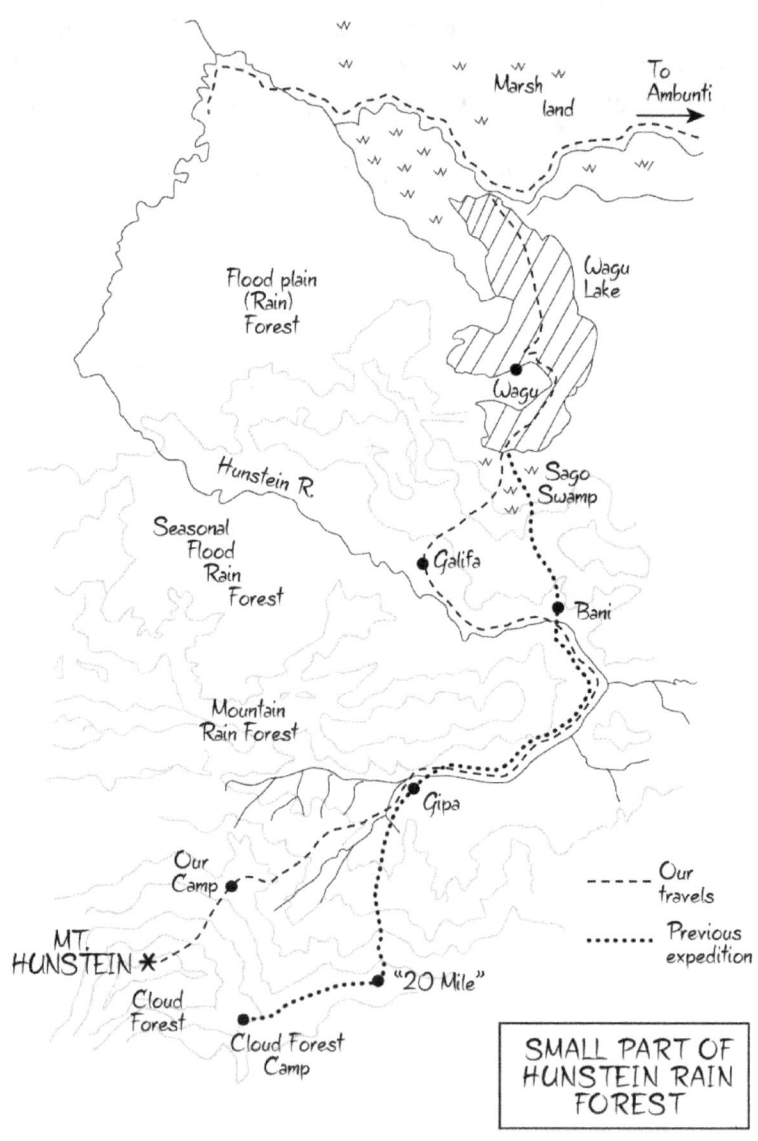

Marsh land

To Ambunti

Flood plain (Rain) Forest

Wagu Lake

Wagu

Hunstein R.

Sago Swamp

Seasonal Flood Rain Forest

Galifa

Bani

Mountain Rain Forest

Gipa

Our Camp

----- Our travels

.... Previous expedition

MT. HUNSTEIN ✳

"20 Mile"

Cloud Forest

Cloud Forest Camp

SMALL PART OF
HUNSTEIN RAIN
FOREST

Chapter 12

A Terrifying Beast

*~~ It stood there, tall and kingly,
taller than me with a dark green cask for a
crown and a huge black body. My father's
ten-gage blasted the world and it turned and
ran. We ran too, until we found it lying
kicking in the mud, another chip away at my
fifteen year old innocence. There was only
one way to bring it home for dinner. My
father and I floated it down the river. The
giant dead beast eyed us underwater at every
turn. ~~*

The leaders talk far into the night. In the morning they are
unanimous. "Some of us should go and look at the route. It can't hurt
anything."

Meanwhile, Max and Karl talk about backing out altogether.

"But you agreed to go as far as cloud forest when you were
hired," I insist.

"If I can't make it, I can't make it," Max answers. "I asked
Wayne and he told me it was a simple four hour hike, and now you
are talking about a whole day."

"But I told you it was an all day hike," I state angrily.
"Wayne lives in the rainforest for months at a time. You can't
compare your walking pace to his."

Max ignores me.

Cloud forest, a phenomenon associated with high tropical
mountains, is quite different from normal rainforests. There, where
clouds hover virtually every day of the year, it never stops being
foggy or rainy, and everything becomes covered in knee high
blankets of moss. Trees are often shorter than down below, since
virtually all true soil has seeped away, but ferns grow everywhere.
High elevations also harbor many different animals, birds and

flowers. This is the refuge of rare and famous birds of paradise. Their loud sharp cry is standard background music, and though they are elusive, their brilliant plumes can, on occasion, be glimpsed somersaulting through the canopy.

Most notable, however, are the nights when the temperatures drop into the forties. Ever present clouds block the light of the moon and stars. Fungi and moss carpet the floor and glow in the dark. Thus it seems to appear as though the world has turned upside down with the "stars" at your feet.

Tiny, rare frogs haunt Mount Hunstein. Each species of frog has a different call. Some sound like baby goats and some sound like doorways creaking open. There are an unbelievable number of different sounds, including those which seem like they are right inside your ear. A certain owl sounds like a woman screaming, and the cries of bats tinkle through the air like shattering crystal glass. No wonder the ancestors were afraid.

"Why don't some of us go up and bring back specimens for Max," Karl suggests. "Max won't make it up that ridge if he can't even hike down here on the flats."

"It'll never work." I say. "The magazine wants pictures of scenery as well as flowers. We especially need to get that fungus which glows at night."

It is pointless to continue the discussion today. Another day in Gipa might give Max a chance to acclimate. Meanwhile, I hope our foray in the new direction will offer a way to cloud forest in half the distance of our original plan.

I shudder to think what would happen if Max didn't get pictures on all the levels of the mountain that *National Geographic* assigned him to take. The magazine is already committed to doing an article about the villagers. But if it leaves the forest part out for lack of pictures, how will readers understand the plight of the forest, or that the villagers and the forest are inextricably connected? Max *must* get up the mountain.

In the morning my Bahinemo friends organize themselves early for our hike. Wamseli and Lekim volunteer to cut a trail. I am to interpret the map. Two women, Moyali and Yamu, and Yamu's small son, Clement, go along in case I need to turn back before the men get tired. Jim and his wife, Bahio, who learned the Western camp routine from the previous expedition, stay behind to take care of the three outsiders, Max, Karl and Rob. Rob is still sunburned and is caught up in reading M.M. Kaye's *Far Pavillions.* He's not in the mood for an extra hike. Ma Jim learned to understand English in the village school, though he very seldom speaks it. He knows quite a bit about Western customs and needs. With food, water, first aid and freshly sharpened machetes, the rest of us start into the forest, heading upriver.

Exotic bird calls echo in the silence of the deep rainforest. Now and then we jump across a stream which cuts through the bank to join the river. The ground is littered with a variety of leaves, fruit and flowers. Sometimes their shapes are bizarre. We find one fruit that bounces and looks like a purple rubber ball. The nuts in the nutmeg family appear to be wrapped with red plastic string. Occasionally we step across a dirty pile of undigested berries and seeds, the scat of the five foot tall, emu-like, fearsome cassowary bird.

Once we catch the smell of a phalanger hidden somewhere in the trees, the small possum-like creature with wide, brown eyes and a rich soft coat which we brought home to the U. S. with us the year before. The forest here is hollow, too sheltered by the dense canopy of leaves far above to provide light for more than some scattered saplings stretching up between the trunks of large trees.

I feel very comfortable, safe and at home. I enjoy the unchanging temperature. I love the feel of the soft dirt and leaves on my bare feet. Usually I prefer to hike barefoot. I know how to use my eyes to read the terrain when I walk in order to find soft places to step. If there are any leeches, being barefoot gives me a chance to feel them and flick them off before they can take hold. Nature, unlike humans, tends to follow patterns one can count on and learn. I feel safe because I know this environment. I know how to avoid danger and am able to relax. I feel a oneness with the beauty, the complexity, the predictability and the awesome power of the living system that surrounds me.

We follow the river for about one hour, across three streams, not two. I am relying on Ma Lekim, and he is relying on me. Several times we leave the trail for a moment and scan the ridge on the opposite side of the river, comparing stories from his ancestral route and my map's elevation lines. This sort of close partnership would have been impossible for those who did not know the language. I begin to understand how the scientists went astray. But for Ma Lekim and me, this is as enjoyable as working on a family jigsaw puzzle. He is in his element and I am in mine. After an hour and a half we both determine at the same time that this is the place to cross the river and cut a trail onto the opposite side.

Lekim seems twenty years younger as acre after acre of familiar earth pass under his feet. When he was a boy, his people lived as nomads, settling in one place with lean-tos until the fruit, leaves and animals in the area were worn thin. Then they would move on. This camp, next to the heart of the world, where the entire world turned cold and the spirits lived, was the farthest camp in their territory. Lekim has longed to be back here since he was a boy. The trek is exactly as he remembers it.

The slope is gentle indeed, though far below we can hear a loud roar as the river crashes and tumbles from the ridges above. The trail we make goes up and up, often coming to places that appear to be the top. A few minutes of scouting always ends up revealing a narrow place to one side or another where the ridge dips slightly and continues on.

At one of these places we stop to rest, and the ladies cut into the bark of the large vine we use as a bench and begin to draw around their wrists with its sticky Elmer's glue-like sap. Later they show me that when it dries and turns clear, it can be rolled off the wrist into very realistic rubber bands. It is a small moment of serendipity.

There seems to be no sure way to gauge how far we have gone, but we know by the valleys on the both sides of the ridge that we are always heading in the right direction. We have been climbing steadily since the moment we left the river. Surely, cloud forest will be just ahead.

This has been such a short, easy trail that I am becoming determined to go to the very top of Mount Hunstein itself!

We travel until 4:00 p.m., when without warning thunder booms out of the depths of the valleys. Mountain storms are almost instantaneous. They tend to regularly flood the river which would make it too hard to cross if we don't return with haste. We run down the mountain in pouring rain.

I marvel at how the women who lead the way remember our trail with absolute accuracy, though only occasional branches have been cut and the whole forest looks the same to me. The way is slippery, and I wonder if Max will be able to make even this trail if the weather turns bad. We lean heavily on walking sticks for balance, swinging ourselves down off the slope from small saplings to lower points on the trail.

I hear loud grunts.

All of my life I have been taught to watch for trees to climb in case of an angry boar or a cassowary. The grunting is coming straight at us in the driving rain. I scream, "Boar!" and hearing me, Moyali grabs at a small tree.

"No. It's a cassowary!" She screams with terror, suddenly seeing the giant bird about five yards ahead. A boar can gore you, but a cassowary might not stop clawing until you are dead. One always imagines that when confronted by a bear or a wild boar or perhaps a cassowary, that the perfect tree will be positioned right alongside the trail. It isn't! Try as I might I can't get up any of the trees that are around me!

The cassowary paws at the ground with its massive claws and grunts with its head down in a charge position. Its rainbow neck glares red to me, in front of its two hundred pounds of menacing black body. We continue to scream and wave our sticks. My legs are trembling so it is hard to stand, let alone climb. At last, the men with the machetes catch up and the giant bird retreats. We run on, rain continuing to pour into our faces.

In forty minutes we re-cover the distance it took us four hours to walk up. We pass out of the rain and reach the river, arriving ahead of both flood and storm. We hurry across and return to camp, tired but elated and disappointed at the same time. Lekim and I have confirmed that this is the correct route to Mount Hunstein. But the only sign of cloud forest we saw was one little frog, and some glow fungus tucked away in my bag. I want more evidence.

5 foot Cassowary Bird and chick

Chapter 13

Black Tuesday

*~~ My little brother, at fourteen, came down
with a terrible attack of malaria on the way to Mt.
Hunstein. Despite his severe nausea, chills, weakness
and fever my father merely redistributed his load. He
couldn't be left behind. ~~*

While Max stayed in camp, he had a change of heart. It
seems the electrolyte drink he agreed to take made a world of
difference. He explored all along the river on the far bank and was
delighted by the scenery there. He decides to try fulfilling his quest
to make it to cloud forest up on the mountain, but first, he wants
another day to photograph Gipa now that he has a feel for it.

Originally, I planned to go right up to the higher camp on
the mountain on Monday. Now we are a day behind. I must adjust
the whole schedule. But, seeing Max so inspired encourages me.
Since he has been resisting going at all, I decide to give Max
Tuesday, our only extra day, to get into the routine. If Max is on a
roll, it seems best to let him continue. Using up our extra day will
give me more time to decide our route. Despite misgivings, I decide
we will all leave Wednesday.

Rob and Max also saw a cassowary early in the morning and
were very excited. "It swam across the river not far from our camp,"
they say. Jim and Bahio caught plenty of catfish for our supper
while we were exploring the mountain and even filleted them
Western style. I fry ours in batter. After some jovial banter the
whole camp goes to bed early. This complacency, however, proves
to be temporary.

Exactly what ruins Tuesday morning is a mystery, but for
one thing, we sleep in late. When I do get up, I decide it is a good
day for pancakes in order to make use of our extra biscuit mix.
Pancakes take a long time to fix. Only Max and Karl have anywhere
to go and they can eat their breakfast first, leaving the rest of us to
eat as the pancakes get done. Biscuit mix is one of the foods I
brought for extra days because it can be made into several things. I

start a fire and begin to mix the batter, only to find that our eggs have spoiled. Without eggs, the biscuit mix sticks to the pan and I have to keep the fire low to keep the pancakes from burning. They are not fried in time for Max.

"What about hot water for my oatmeal and coffee?" he demands. "At least I expect to be able to get hot water when I need it!" I look around, but the only water is cold. He is furious. Then he starts to yell.

"Every expedition I have ever been on had hot water for coffee every morning," Max hollers. "And on this one you don't even have a set time for meals. Furthermore, why haven't your carriers built me a table?" he asks, fists clenched. "It seems to me that if they can make shelves and beds, they could easily make a table!" Rob and I look at each other in shock. We never even thought of a table, we confess. "You mean you brought me out here and you are not even thinking about the simplest considerations? Here we are eating like animals!"

The carriers flinch with fear and horror.

What a change from Max's old good-humored response to inconvenience, "That should be your biggest problem."

Rob gets angry. He doesn't like anyone referring to ours or the carriers' ways as "like animals". For a minute I fear they might come to blows. We are quite comfortable sitting on logs around a campfire with our plates on our laps. Yet, as I think about it, I realize most of American socialization occurs around a table at meals. Of course, the rest of us find plenty of fellowship every evening around the campfire. Max, however, finds sitting so low to the ground next to who-knows-what six-legged item in the dark most uncomfortable. And he does not speak the language. We have been discussing everything in a mixture of Tok Pisin (trade language), and Bahinemo. I am getting more and more comfortable in both languages. Even Rob and Karl can at least understand Tok Pisin. Max has indeed been greatly neglected.

Clearly issues for Max have been building up with no chance to resolve them, although I have been too busy to notice. I have, in fact, lost touch with all sense of schedule, having switched to my Papua New Guinea side almost completely. No doubt Max is experiencing classic culture shock. It probably hasn't occurred to him that we are providing time for discussion and pulling the group together. In fact he has been skipping our times around the campfire and going straight to bed. I think he needs an interpreter, not a table.

More things are said, regretted by all, until it comes down to the point that Max doesn't trust me for two reasons, and has consequently been feeling more and more insecure: First, I confess to often thinking like a Bahinemo and using their logic to make decisions, which according to his view is a lot less rational and developed. Secondly, I ignored the advice of the Westerners and chose carriers who were "my friends." We are unable to ease his fears. I don't regret my actions, but it helps him to at least recognize the real source of his tension. I assure him again and again that I have chosen the best team available.

As to his expressive outburst, Max informs us that he feels no shame as he has always been taught that it's best to get your feelings out rather than to let things build up. This is a very legitimate constructive cultural trait… in New York. The Bahinemos however, find it appalling.

In the end it turns out that Jim and Bahio did get up early that morning, as they have every morning to make hot water for Max's coffee, but since Max slept in, the water got cold. Jim understands Max's angry words, but is too embarrassed to mention these efforts until after the argument is over. He is offended. He has made this his daily practice for the sole purpose of pleasing Max. He is not Max's slave. He was hired to carry, not to serve. He knows some Westerners like or even need hot coffee every morning, but it doesn't occur to him that someone besides the Westerners themselves might be obliged to provide it. He doesn't know that provision of coffee is expected in other parts of the world. He has been boiling water in the morning just because he cares.

There is no comprehension of servitude in Bahinemo culture. There are men's and women's roles, but no one human being is ever expected to make another happy because of his or her position. Unlike Western cultures which contain a hierarchy of job positions, or many third world cultures with their histories of repression, in Bahinemo culture all men are truly equal.

It is lunch before I finish making the pancakes. No one feels like eating them anyway.

In the afternoon, Rob and I cross the river to where Ma Lekim helps Max and Karl photograph some carnivorous pitcher plants near a beautiful waterfall. The exquisite little pots are similar to venus fly traps, but they hang from vines at a variety of levels. Golden sun rays shine down through the canopy.

Max has his tripod set up and is framing some wonderful vignettes. One thing I really appreciate about him is that he looks closely at the tiny things many people wouldn't notice. Therein lies so much of the beauty of the rainforest. Seen at a distance, all is green. Up close, there are amazing patterns, colors, adaptations and variations, in an unimaginable assortment, scattered everywhere. This is what we have brought Max into the rainforest to do.

Rob and I explored the waterfall last year, only to be told that in so doing, we had offended spirits and caused the violent thunderstorm and lightning which had struck the camp hours later. It seemed a certain man had once been killed up on that very ridge. His body had been tossed into the creek above the falls. No one had ever gone there since, until the two of us explored it and found wonderful tiers of alternating cascades and round, bubbling pools carved in limestone. At river level the falls pound through a cave-like canyon, which seems impassable. But, there is a way around it.

While Ma Lekim waits to help Max move his camera equipment to the next site, he follows me to the edge of the falls. "It's beautiful, isn't it, San Lekim?" he exclaims quietly to me, using "San" for "Mrs." and calling me "Lekim" to refer to our close relationship just as I do to him. "Look, there are two whole separate falls, one up there and one falling into the cave," he marvels. "Isn't that where you and Rob swam when everyone said you caused the storm?"

"Oh no," I reply. "These are only the first two falls. There are many more. Where we swam was much higher."

"Really?" He asks with awe in his voice. "You really went up there? I wonder what it looks like. Which way did you go?" The falls appear to be blocked by sheer cliffs, but we are standing only a few feet from a brush hidden man-sized crevice that I know leads right to the creek above it.

"Why, it's right here," I answer. "You just go through these rock walls. It's very close. You could look if you like." He takes in a deep breath and peers at me as a boy would on a dare. He has told me he believes that since I am a Christian, I am safe from the spirit in the falls. He too is a Christian, so he has no real excuse not to stand by that premise for himself. Papua New Guinea villagers often turn to Christianity with its promise of a God who is more powerful than their rampant evil spirits. Now his curiosity drives him to test his new beliefs. I don't want to add to this pressure, so I change the subject, but Karl, an agnostic, is listening.

"You're afraid of the spirits aren't you?" Karl teases the older man. "I don't believe in spirits at all. I have lived many years and have never seen even one," Karl scoffs, showing the contempt for the old ways often found in Papua New Guineans with a strong Western education.

Ma Lekim edges closer to the narrow crevice. "Here, I'll take you up," I volunteer, seeing his longing. This is a statement I will come to regret more than any other thing I say or do on the entire expedition.

Ma Lekim sets down his bag and steps toward the rock wall, but hesitates one more time. "I'll pray for you for protection if you like," I assure him, thinking it will calm his nerves.

"Oh yes, please do," he says, so I do. He thrusts himself up and forward into the crevice. He is staring at a whole series of cascades carved out of rock. "They're beautiful!" he exclaims. "I had no idea there was so much here. Come on. Let's go have a look." I scramble up after him, and we both lower ourselves into the roaring creek and begin to climb the slippery rock faces.

Up and up we go, skirting imaginatively shaped pools and tumbling musical cascades of water. When Lekim has gone quite high, he turns to see me, but I am lagging behind. I am hesitating, thinking that Rob is missing out. I can see Rob swimming in the pool below the main waterfall so I stop and motion to him to come up. Ma Lekim sees me, but doesn't understand my motioning. He interprets my waving arms and staying so far below as a warning of imminent danger. Lekim rushes back down, fear enveloping his face. When he gets back to where I am, I explain that I was motioning for Rob, but he has had enough. He rushes down the last rock face, back toward the crevice. I hold my breath, thinking of how slippery the last rock is. But, I soothe myself; he has had many more years of experience with slippery rocks than I have. Sure enough, he makes it.

Then, Rob and I hear a sickening yell. Ma Lekim has fallen on his way out of the creek. He is only six inches from a twenty foot precipice. His face is frozen with terror. I rush down the rock to meet him and see that he has dislocated his big toe. Blood pours out of his shin in three places. The water turns red.

Rob and I cradle him in our arms and pray again, this time in earnest and with considerably shaken faith. Rob grabs Lekim's toe and yanks. It realigns. Trembling ourselves, we manage to help him back through the crevice, down the path and back across the river to camp. I bandage the wounds snugly and give him Tylenol. There is no ice for his toe. He lays in a hammock as stiff as a corpse for the next five hours. It is no use trying to blame the accident on fear. I apologize over and over. Finally he pats my arm and says, "San Edie, You did not force me to go there." --A small comfort.

There is no question in my mind that I must stay in Gipa until I am satisfied that Ma Lekim's injuries will not require an evacuation. His cuts are healing well, but his toe is huge and the pain is severe so there is nothing for him to do but lay still. His depression is deeper and more morose than any I have ever seen, and he does not move or speak. Among other things, he is devastated by the thought that after all these years he could come so close and yet not see the mountain of his youth once again.

"Black Tuesday", we might call it. That night, everyone goes to bed early.

Chapter 14

Fishing

~~ "Come on!" my brothers yelled in unison. "We've got the poison vine. Come help us catch fish. It's fun." We did and it was. The Bahinemo boys helped my brothers dam up a stream. Then they pounded the vine with rocks and swished it in the pool. Up came the fish and slam went the machetes and sticks. We gathered armfuls of stunned little fish. The boys threaded them on a spear and we had more than we could eat. ~~

Wednesday, the day we are supposed to leave, there is nothing to do but rest. Karl does not pass up the opportunity to remind me that Lekim's accident wouldn't have happened had I not taken an older man in the first place. I can only kick myself for our careless little frolic.

I decide to spend most of the day accompanying Ma Jim and the two boys, Mathew and Clement, spear fishing on the river. Rob is still not ready to get back in the sun. Besides, he is so lost in "Far Pavilions" he might as well be in India, where the book takes place. Between the sunburn, the captivating book and the ever present language barrier, he doesn't feel much like being active in the group, so I invite San Bahio. She is delighted to join me. We make sure all the camp chores are done and everything is at peace. Then we set off to find the guys.

The two of us follow the old, dry river bed, skipping from rock to rock so as not to burn our bare feet. Soon it joins the main river and shade. This is the first time Bahio and I have a chance to catch up on our friendship.

San Bahio is about eighteen years old and is not, in fact, a true Bahinemo though her culture is almost identical to theirs. Bahio is short and round for a Bahinemo, and thus beautiful in their eyes. Like Moyali, she came from the next language group over, the Kagiru, when she was young. Bahio and Jim met at the government basic school, and fell in love. She understands Bahinemo rather well, but is more comfortable in Tok Pisin. Since they speak Tok Pisin to each other at home, they are both better communicators with outsiders than most.

Bahio's home village is farther back in the forest than Wagu and has less access to civilization. Her father demanded a high bride price of Ma Jim who could speak some English and find occasional work. The amount was so high it would take Jim years to pay. Instead of waiting, the two eloped. Ma Jim is still being pressured to earn the money and pay the full price, but meanwhile, at least he and Bahio are together. Both are highly independent, intelligent, motivated and goal oriented, but what stands out most is their excitement about life.

We cover the route deep in conversation about happenings in Wagu and about my children whom she babysat the year before. I am now out of contact with them for the first time in their lives. I feel a pang of guilt for leaving them and a longing to know how they are faring. After a long while we spot Bahio's husband and the two boys lounging at the edge of a large, picturesque water hole.

The Bahinemo men and the two boys have worked their way up the river each day since we arrived, targeting the big pools one at a time for catfish. I saw this particular pool two days earlier when we went to scout the new trail up the mountain. Looking down from the high bank across the river we saw schools of two and a half foot long catfish milling around and around in the bottom of a deep basin.

As Bahio and I arrive, the fishermen are sunning themselves on rocks, getting warm and waiting for the fish to settle before stirring them up again with their spears. The water is crystal clear and the fish stay in the pool like gold fish in a bowl, bordered as it is by rapids upstream and down. Several large catfish have already been caught. Jim wears Western goggles and brandishes a long spear, and the guys plan to stay at this pool for a few more hours. Ma Jim jumps up happily to greet us when he sees us coming.

While we join their wait, they point to the trail above the cliff opposite us and inform me they are also keeping an eye out for Ma Gogomo who said he would join them on his way back from the advanced camps of the previous expedition. He left early that morning, they tell me, to try and retrieve some tarps which the scientists left behind. I am disturbed because he had not told me anything about this dangerous undertaking. Nor did we need any more tarps.

Gogomo amazes me that he would attempt a round trip all the way up the difficult trail the Bahinemos describe as like "climbing trees" to camp "20 mile," in one day. Very few Bahinemos would venture far into the forest alone, let alone on such a strenuous mission. Ma Gogomo is so much stronger, braver and self-sacrificing than normal people that he has become a legend, and few even attempt to follow his pastoral example. They view him as one made of different stuff. He can do the work of any three men at one time. But I know since he went without telling me, he is not happy with the way things are going. Something is brewing and I don't like it.

I brought along a disposable underwater camera, hoping to bring back pictures of the big catfish in their natural state. The pool is in the shade of a gigantic tree and the water is too cold for me, so I let Jim be the photographer, which he loves. He dives way down right into the catfishes' midst. After going down so deep, he too is cold, so he hands the camera to me and goes back to fishing from the surface. He hangs onto a floating log and peers through his worn, old pair of diving goggles, spear poised. The goggles let in water every few minutes, and he has to adjust them, but this hassle is worth the view they give of the fish circling below. After about five minutes, Jim jabs his long spear forward and brings a flip-flopping specimen to the surface.

I rush forward into the water to photograph the moment and my culottes billow instantly up around my waist, leaving me rather inappropriately exposed. We all roar with laughter and I decide to join Bahio in declining swimming for the rest of the event.

Bahinemo standards of modesty forbid women to wear pants or bathing suits. It is rare for women to swim with men, for fear of just such incidents.

Bahio climbs up the rocks to the rapids above the falls where nine year old Clement is staring into the water with his little spear poised and ready. "Come on!" she yells to me. "He's found a fish up here! We can round it up and catch it." I wonder how one can see a fish in such frothy water, and am a little surprised to learn catfish can do well in a current. "Sometimes they jump right up a waterfall," Bahio says.

Sure enough, when I reach the spot, I can clearly make out a swiveling blue gray shadow where everyone is pointing into the heavy current. The sun shines onto the large stones in the riverbed below it, reflecting many other shades of lighter gray, red and brown so the fish is well camouflaged. No wonder I have never recognized a catfish in a rapids before.

Bahio runs back to the pool to call her husband, and asks him to bring his heavier spear. Meanwhile, Clement makes jabs with his short one, frightening the fish a few feet farther up the river. At one point it hovers only three feet away from me so I hold my camera below the surface and hit the button.

Soon Ma Jim, Clement and Mathew clamber back and forth, up and down the rapids, aiming their spears. Their supple bare feet cling and balance on loose rocks in the river bed as they run. Bahio brandishes a machete. I stand on a high rock nearby and join in, shouting directions whenever the fish can only be seen from my position. As the fish swims to and fro, everyone yells out cheers and instructions.

"Here it comes!"

"Bahio, it's going for you!"

"Oh, oh, there it goes now, to the left. The left!"

"Let me at it, I can reach it from here."

Bahio plunges her hands into the water, but it dashes through her legs and zooms over to a different spot. Jim sees it and edges over quickly. We hold our breath. Suddenly he lunges forward clutching his spear, but the fish escapes and is seen hurling downstream to where young Clement is waiting.

Clement yells. He throws rocks. He clutches his child's spear and strains his eyes.

"Clement! Clement! You can do it! You can do it. Catch it!" we all cheer.

Suddenly the fish turns and heads back upstream. "Jim, quick, it's heading for the rocks!" Mathew yells. Jim moves in stealthily. We hold our breath again. He creeps to within two feet of the lively, gray shadow. In a flash, his spear thrusts forward and he holds up another flip-flopping cat. A quick slap with Bahio's machete and the fish no longer feels defeat.

Suddenly it strikes me that this fish hunt is exactly like our Western ball games.

The chase, the catch, the cheering and the thrill are all identical. Are these things in our blood, common to all cultures?

I begin to think of other similarities between our two cultures. The closer I look, the more differences seem like similarities.

I recall the way the women who brought me down the mountain in the rain, raced over a trail we had only just invented. What were they observing? Wasn't it tiny differences in the forest, lost to those untrained to recognize exactly what is ordinary and what isn't? Could they be noticing crooked trees, for example, or special vines? Could this be the same process by which some people in Western society find it easy to tell which fashions are new each year and which are old? With years of experience, they are able to tell what aspects of this year's clothing styles are different from last year's.

I, caught between cultures, have never mastered either. I haven't the faintest clue whether it is the shape of the collar which counts this year, or the number of buttons. I have no idea what to look for.

The sun lowers in the sky, indicating we have been fishing for several hours. I am tempted to disbelieve the sun as it seems as if only a few minutes have passed. We head slowly back to camp, checking small pools for elusive eels, savoring our last moments to fish.

In the evening I am plagued with the need to decide for sure which of three ways we should head in the morning; the old, steep, long way where Gogomo is now, the new unexplored way that seems right on the map, or one in the middle. We are already far behind schedule. There is no more room for contingencies. "Is there a set altitude where one will find cloud forest?" I ask Karl.

Karl assures me there is. "By 900 meters at least, we should reach that type of forest no matter what else the mountain is like." he says. Karl was chosen for his experience with PNG forests and his scientific knowledge of their plants. I am confident we can reach that altitude easily by the new route. By the old route, I know it would take a day and a half. By the new route we might reach the very top of the mountain in that length of time.

"What about water?" Karl wants to know. "Did you see any water up there while scouting the new trail?" We hadn't, but after a few moments of thought Karl answers his own question by determining there is always water in a rainforest, even if it must be derived from puddles rather than a creek. "No, it can't be a serious problem," he decides, "though it might present an inconvenience."

Quite apart from the matter of which trail to take, is the question of how to get anywhere at all with one carrier wounded. The villagers won't hear of leaving Ma Lekim alone. Just the suggestion produces shocked and offended expressions. Instead they propose some of them carry our things up for the day and return to Gipa at night. We could send a party down ahead to summon them when we need to return, or they could just go back up the mountain on a certain day and meet us.

This wonderful idea solves many problems: We are able to subtract the bedding and supplies of the carriers who will travel round trip from the overall load. The camp here at Gipa will not have to be packed up and stored. Max can leave his extra cameras here under Ma Lekim's watchful eye, further lightening the load. There would be fewer people to feed, as the ones left behind would have nothing required of them and could be free to find fish, collect the starch of the sago palm, and gather leaves and fruits.

The only concern left is leaving Ma Lekim alone for the day of the hike. I decide Ma Lekim's wounds are painful but not life threatening. Finally it is decided that nine year old Clement is old enough to be officially hired as a little watchman. I agree to pay Clement for this so he will take it seriously.

It appears at last there are no more obstacles to our leaving. Everyone tensely awaits my decision about the direction we will go.

Gogomo does not return until supper is served at dark. Clearly he is exhausted. As soon as he arrives, I inundate him with questions about the old trail. He ignores me. I pause and look around at the others, then select one question and put it forth carefully. He wolfs down another mouthful of food.

I feel embarrassed when I remember that to talk while you are eating is quite rude in Bahinemo culture. I started the discussion before the evening fire time while we were still eating, so as to include Max and Karl. The other Bahinemos are putting up with this under the circumstances. Maybe the man is too tired to deal with such cultural compromises. Still, I have a feeling something is wrong.

Later around the campfire, Ma Gogomo describes his trip in rapid Bahinemo slang with a lot of words from Bahio's language thrown in. I can only catch the gist of the conversation, giving me a taste of Rob, Max and Karl's daily frustrations. I decide Gogomo is trying to leave me out on purpose; further evidence he is angry with me, but he refuses to admit so, or to talk about it. Jim and Bahio translate some things.

"The old trail is very, very difficult," Gogomo says. "I don't think everyone will make it. It took me many hours. It is completely overgrown and will have to be re-cut."

At this point almost all of the carriers want me to take the middle route, including Gogomo. This is the trail Wayne created at the end of the last expedition, in his attempt to find the real way up. Those who went up it then assure me it is much easier than "20 mile" and also leads to cloud forest. But they think it will take even longer than "20 mile". I try to get them to describe the forest at the level where we would camp. "Was it a cold place?" I ask. "Was there moss on the trees and glow fungus at night?" Answers are varied and unsure.

No one has talked about the new route since Lekim's fall, and I wonder if they are avoiding it for his sake, since he can no longer go.

On the surface, the middle trail does seem like a compromise between steepness and the unknown new route on the aerial map. But when I take a closer look, I find the middle route contains as many unknowns as the new route. The forest type of the middle camp is in question. The distance from there to cloud forest is in question. Water on it is scarce, so that hardship is certain. And compared with our new trail, it is still quite steep and long.

The pressure is intense. I must find a way to get Max at least as far as cloud forest. The mountain is tempting me and I also long to get to the top of it, though admittedly that was not the express requirement of the magazine. Our real purpose is to bring the rainforest to the world at various levels so readers might fall in love with it. However, I believe if we take the new route, the top will only be a one day round trip away from our higher level camp.

At the end of the discussion, quite late in the evening, Ma Lekim speaks at last. It is the first time he has said anything to the group since the fall. His words are short and simple.

"You must take the new route, San Edie." he says firmly. "It is the route of our ancestors and it will be the shortest way. Even though I cannot go, you must go for me. You will find the lake and then you will all know that I speak the truth."

The embers of the campfire flicker slowly, casting an orange glow into the shadows of a dark night. Somewhere, a small branch drops from a tree, momentarily breaking the heavy silence. There are no more words from anyone.

San Bahio

Fishing with machete

A fish caught with a spear

2 foot catfish at bottom of pool

Chapter 15

The Carriers Sit

*~~ I drove a boatload of people
through the swamp at age eighteen. Grass
islands closed in behind us. We were trapped.
I needed someone to lift the engine so I could
plow the boat through the gaps in the tall
grass. No one moved.~~*

Sometime in the middle of the night I wake up to thunder.
Water is pouring over the tent as if water bags above the forest are
leaking. In the distance I hear the roar and crash of a tree falling and
shudder. For a while, I just listen to the pounding rain. I feel around
the tent to see what is wet. I find only drops from condensation.
Then I hear a trickling sound.

What begins as a simple melodious trickle, cheering the roar
of the storm, grows quickly to a babble somewhere near the tent.
Soon it sounds like water is raging all around us. I decide to step
outside to check the camp but when I unzip the tent door a crack,
water sprays in and the beam of my flashlight shows bare ground.
Perhaps it isn't as bad as it sounds. I wiggle down farther into my
sleeping bag and doze off.

In the morning there is a creek to wade between our tents
and the carriers' shelter. From the way small plants are pushed over
it appears it was three feet deep at its peak. The only places back in
the forest where we Westerners stayed which are not inundated are
the two tiny spots where Ma Lekim had firmly instructed me to put
our platforms. Not one item or person is wet on those two platforms;
one of Ma Lekim's "secrets of the forest."

We pass out granola and some of us start to pack. One way
or the other we have to leave today. We are running out of food. Off
and on the rain continues, but it looks as if it might go away by
noon.

The carriers sit.

By ten o'clock most of our supplies are ready, but the carriers still have not taken down even one of their own tents. Karl and Max are becoming furious at their refusal to help. Even Rob and I are exasperated. Finally I order them to take down the tents. They stare at me with stunned silence and grudgingly begin to move.

"Okay, guys. What's going on?" I demand.

Wamseli finally speaks, "If we go up that new trail in this rain, we'll have to come back down when the river is flooded. We might not make it back across," he says.

"Alright," I reply, "but you could have told me that earlier. Something else is going on around here, and someone needs to let me in on it." They ignore this last statement.

"Are you going to make us go now, risking danger to our wives and our children?" the carriers ask.

I hate this, "Are you going to make us…" imperialistic stuff. I know their judgment is sounder than ours when it comes to trails.

Just then, Karl speaks up. "Max is getting good pictures around here. He isn't wasting his time. How much food do we have left?"

"Enough to make this our last delay," I reply. "If we have any more delays, there is some emergency rice and cheese, but otherwise, we have enough supplies left to spend two days on the mountain and two at Bani." Bani is the last camp where we need to stop. It's downriver, back toward the village of Wagu. We will pass it on our way out of the rainforest. We are supposed to collect a few photos of seasonal flood plain forest there.

"Why don't we just do one day at Bani?" Karl suggests. "The guys and I will go up the mountain by the new trail today, farther than you and Solomon (Ma Lekim) went. We'll locate a campsite with water. This will minimize the risks for a final attempt tomorrow."

Perhaps another preliminary trek would assuage everyone's fears about the new route, I think. Then maybe they will work with one mind. But there are always contingencies. I can only imagine what might happen at our next two stops if we can't even get away from here. I realize we are in serious danger of running out of food, but if I make the carriers go against their will, I will lose our important bond.

It doesn't look like the carriers are ready to take a load anywhere while the river is still somewhat flooded from the night before. The men, at least, could swim back across in the rain. Gogomo, Wamseli, Jim and Karl leave at noon with no loads. They go to further scout out the new trail Ma Lekim and the map say we should take. We will leave Friday.

The sun comes out almost as soon as they leave. This last delay has been a mistake.

Rob invites me to explore some new creeks with him alone, and it seems a welcome respite. Max busies himself cleaning equipment. This is down time for all of us.

Because the river is flooded and we want to keep our clothes dry, Rob and I cut across a new stretch of forest. As soon as we enter the twilight, emerald cathedral, we spot a little wallaby hopping by about 100 feet away. We freeze and he freezes too, cocking his soft head to look us over. Then he is off.

After a short while we come to the part of the river which leads to the creek we intend to explore. We have to cross the river to get there, and it is flooded, though the water level is going down quickly. No one is around, so this time, in order to keep our clothes dry we take them off and hold them above our heads to wade. The sun is now shining bright and warm. Birds and butterflies have redecorated the world with music and color in full force. Sandbars are rising, freshly combed, out of the current; some slightly rearranged from the night before. We feel like Adam and Eve.

On the other side of the river fresh cassowary tracks fill us with wonder and apprehension. The tracks measure a foot across from toe to toe. The huge bird must have disappeared just moments before. Our hearts beat faster as we contemplate what to do if he is only a few yards away. As we enter the forest on the other side, however, we don't see him. Every moment that goes by makes us feel a little safer. If the bird is near, he should have seen us by now and moved. Cassowaries only attack when cornered or startled.

We wade up the far side of the river to the creek. This we follow until we have discovered and played in several small waterfalls and pools. Then we return to camp. No insects, water-soaked nights, tired limbs, or unusual rations, could ever begin to mar my love for this place!

The only ones at camp for a light soup lunch are San Bahio, the two boys, Mathew and Clement, Rob, Max and myself. Lekim is not hungry and ambles to the river to put his foot in cool water. After eating, the men take naps, and Bahio entertains the boys and me with legends.

She begins with stories about cassowaries. There are several. The first one tells how a man jumps behind a tree when a cassowary attacks and it attacks the tree instead. The bird gets one of its six-inch claws stuck in the wood, so the hunter promptly kills it and brings it home for supper.

From cassowaries Bahio goes on to python stories. These culminate in one where an old lady who is wrapped in a python as long as a house fakes her death, so the python sets her down to go get a drink before his meal. She flees for her life, but her village does not believe her, so she goes back to the snake with a bag of warm water. This she places where the snake had left her body hours before. The snake comes along and thinking the bag is her, wraps itself around it. Then the woman leaps upon it with her machete and chops it all to pieces. In the stories, sometimes the humans live and sometimes they die. Unlike our tales where the outcome is clear from the beginning, you never know who will win, the animal or the human.

There are several versions of the "warm water bag" theme including those which fool not only snakes, but also cassowaries, enemy humans and especially wilderness trolls. These, she says, are little men with bushy beards who always attempt to trick people. Sometimes women who are tricked are never heard from again. What suspense! One thing seems clear: the only way to escape a troll's menace, is to outfox it more than it outfoxes you.

After a while Bahio wonders aloud if her husband up on the mountain might be looking for trolls. Mount Hunstein, most sacred and central of all the mountains, is considered to be prime stomping ground for trolls. It is also thought to be haunted by an old Japanese man who, so the story goes, ran to Mt. Hunstein and hid after World

War II. One story says he killed his wife and threw her in the mysterious lake.

Bahio dozes off. The boys and I sit gazing at the fire. I marvel at the way she can sleep while flies buzz over her skin. I think about the Japanese men who did hide out in the war. Wouldn't they be in their 70's by now? It is hot, and I wish more than anything we would have all been off, up on the mountain ourselves. We are wasting time.

About mid-afternoon, San Moyali comes into camp loaded with berries, fruit and leaves. She was out making sago and ran across several tasty favorites. Moyali arranges the various leaves, each more tender than spinach, into groups, and covers them with large, tough "cooking" leaves. She steams these packets on the fire. Then Moyali lays out a type of fig, which the kids gobble up at once, and some little red cherry-like fruits. When Bahio wakes up and sees the red berries, she begs to know the source of them. Soon Rob, Bahio, the boys and I follow Moyali into the forest and down the river to the berry tree. They are very tart and I think they might make a good dessert if we had extra sugar.

Karl has been complaining we aren't getting enough vegetables. The vegetables we are eating are freeze-dried Western peas and beans, which never quite regain their former shapes. Moyali and Yamu make a delicious soup with the leaves and seeds of the salt tree. Considering we are running low on food, I decide to try and serve this soup with rice and mackerel for a change from our usual Western diet. I, at least, find it delicious.

Max is incensed. He complains bitterly, asserting that nothing I promised in meals materialized. It is tempting to abandon him here at base camp with Ma Lekim, but I force myself to keep in mind that he is the sole reason for our trip and that it's my job to see that he gets to each type of forest and back. It doesn't occur to me that Europeans would find it awkward to keep spitting large seeds out of their soup every few minutes.

At dusk the men stagger back to camp.

Around the fire, they all tell their stories at once. Shortly after the place where Lekim and I turned back, they indeed discovered a lake. Set into the side of the ridge, it appeared completely unnatural. At that point the ridge was only four feet wide and dropped steeply on either side. The lake hung twenty feet straight down on one side. Its water was terribly stagnant, with no apparent way to escape the pocket. All in all, the "lake" was about thirty yards in diameter, and bordered by palms at its lip as Ma Lekim predicted. Hidden by trees, it could have escaped aerial photographs from which my topographical map was made.

Jim got sick just looking at it. He became nauseated and his head has ached ever since. He contends it is either altitude sickness, or the magic of the lake itself. Fearing the worst, I check him for signs of malaria but he has no fever. Instead, I treat him for dehydration. He did not drink all day, he admits. The men didn't find water until they got to the lake and he certainly couldn't touch that! He felt too sick to go any further. Wamseli waited with him there until the other two returned.

Gogomo and Karl found water an hour farther up the ridge. There was a tiny creek there and a place we could camp. The two men had walked beyond that until they came to a "thousand foot cliff."

"Wait a minute," I say. "There are no 'thousand foot cliffs' on the topographical map."

"Well the map must be wrong," Karl informs me. "We could see without any doubt the mountain is opposite a great chasm, the bottom of which is filled with rushing rivers."

I am completely baffled. I recheck the map. There are no chasms anywhere on it. The ridge proceeds steadily to the top.

Further questioning leads only to some mumbling about "the way mountains are always shaped." I am quite certain the men must have stood on a high point and looked at the ridge across the valley instead of the primary peak. A drop of up to a hundred feet might not be recognized by the topographical lines on my map. The heights of the trees could further affect the aerial analysis by a few meters, but no more than that. As far as visibility from the ground, such a drop could easily disappear into the surrounding trees.

No longer does it enter my mind that the new trail might be venturing in the wrong direction. I have absolute confidence the trail we have been scouting fits the map to perfection. I am quite sure this is our short cut to high altitudes.

My biggest problem now is I have lost the confidence of scientist, Karl. He no longer believes in the new route and is convinced it leads to a dead end. His training hasn't included experience with topographical maps. Even scientists trained with topographical maps seem to find it difficult to apply them to the tropical field. But the Bahinemos respect Karl as they do me. His doubts make them confused.

I haven't yet figured out what was bothering the carriers earlier, but I won't find out anything from the tired men this night. My firm plan is to lead the expedition up the new route in the morning.

It rains all night. In the morning the river is flooded, just as the day before. The sky is gray. Once again the carriers just sit there. We are at the end of our schedule. We will leave today or not at all. I am beginning to think God doesn't want us to go.

Midmorning I ask Gogomo to follow me to the river for a private chat. "What's on your mind?" I ask. "You were angry at me the other night, but you said nothing." He still says nothing. We stand for a while. Then we both admire some little bean sprouts, three inches high, which Bahio planted as seeds two nights before. I wait.

At last he knows I really want his opinion. "San Edie, it's like this," he begins. "Last Sunday, you never held church. You all went on working as if it were a regular week day.

"All of us have talked it over, and we believe you did wrong. When we first came we were ready to hike. Now we have been delayed day after day. We do not think God is happy now. If you had rested that day, you would have seen the wisdom of going straight up the mountain while everyone was fresh."

"Is that everything the carriers are saying?" I ask him.

"Yes it is." he replies.

I don't know what comes over me. I don't normally believe God manipulates us like that, but for whatever reason, on the spot, I think he's right. Maybe it's because I certainly have no explanation for our unending string of misfortunes. All I can do is apologize: "I did not want to offend those in camp who are of other religions," I explain to him. Gogomo seems to view this as a lame excuse instead of a true confession but decides to pray for us.

When I get back to camp, I apologize to the carriers for "chickening out" and not holding a service or letting them have the whole day off because I knew my co-workers did not believe in such things. I explain we will have to go on from here and do the best we can, and that Gogomo has prayed for us. I tell them that because it is our last chance to go, in spite of the rain, we will leave immediately, and if the river is not low enough to cross by the time we get to it, we will go up the old trail.

The sun comes out at once. Everyone grins. The camp is packed in less than an hour.

We start up the trail in a long straggling line. We have made a serious effort to lighten our load, but even so, there is too much. Karl, Rob and I still have to carry packs.

Rob, Jim, Bahio and I are at the end of the entourage. I carry Jim and Bahio's bilum string bag filled with their personal gear because it is fairly light and I know I am out of shape. The handle of the bilum loops over my forehead in traditional Bahinemo fashion, leaving the bulky loaded string bag to hang down my back. It has been a long time since I have kept my balance carrying the full weight of a load with my head in this manner. It feels good, but I wonder how many of my childhood muscles have atrophied.

Everything goes along fine until we have to climb over a large, slippery log. I am right behind Rob, keeping a methodical pace. I expect him to jump down the other side of the log. Instead, he stops just as I reach the top and swings around to see me, slamming the steel tripod strapped to the back of his pack, into my temples. I find myself lying on soggy ground with a good view of bugs, dead leaves and molds, and a serious headache. So much for carrying a string bag with my head! I trade with Bahio for the heavy camera pack she is carrying.

We reach the river in less than forty-five minutes. It is clear and almost back to its normal level. The sun is still shining, and we cross easily. We take the new route. The four carriers who are to make a round trip back to Gipa want to go on ahead. We tell them to find a good place near the small creek we are to camp at and leave our things there under a tarp in case it rains. They say good-bye and disappear into the trees ahead of us.

To the occasional loud, plaintive "Woa, woa, woa" of a bird-of-paradise calling in higher and higher notes, and the distant roar of rivers, we climb slowly and steadily up the ancestral story trail.

At one point we come across a small fire. We assume it must belong to the carriers who went ahead of us.

By the time we get to the lake, we are exhausted and silent. I take one look, and feel both nausea and a reoccurrence of my headache. Is this my imagination? The lake is dark and eerie; a crater, indeed clinging to the side of the ridge. Though it lies just twenty feet down from the ridge top where we stand, not one person even considers approaching it. Strange plants cling to its far side, including sago palms normally found in swamps. I wonder what on earth holds it there.

We pass the return carriers and plod on. There are times when, because of our loads, we feel like we can go no further. At one such place we stop for about twenty minutes. "I simply can't go on," Max says. "Perhaps we could stop here and the carriers could go ahead to find the rest of our gear and bring it back. It will be dark in an hour."

"There's no water here for a camp," Karl points out. Our eyes all move to a muddy puddle which wild pigs have dug, and mentally we taste it.

"Come on," Rob says, "One's destination is nearly always a few feet from the very place where one truly gives up." I think he has read too many novels, but I put on my pack and start forward. Our gear is only one hundred feet up the trail.

Chapter 16

A Thousand Foot Chasm

*~~ We faced a dilemma. Our compass
and topographical map did not agree. We
kids wanted to follow the map which directed
us up a ridge. Dad insisted on the compass
and was soon lost in swamp. We had to go
back and rescue him. Later it was learned
that the compass had been thrown off by the
metal in the mountain.~~*

The men set up the tents and jungle hammocks. Bahio and I
gather water and firewood, and then make tuna casserole in a pot.
We assemble an efficient camp in less than an hour. We serve
supper and secure everything before dark for the inevitable rain.

Rob and I decide that sleep will be more blessed without the
stickiness and mud from a day of hiking. As soon as we are through
eating, we stumble and feel our way with flashlights down the side
of the ridge to the tiny trickle of a creek. The two steep sides of the
beginning of a ravine protect us from view from the camp. We pick
our way with care over rough, mineral laden shale looking for a pool
large enough to sit in. Finally, we move some small rocks and make
one.

Such tiny, stable creeks must exist only in rainforests. We
are right at the creek's very source, yet it flows steadily. It sustains
many small shrimp which Bahio and I labored to remove from the
drinking bucket. (We trust our filter system to remove everything
else.)

Now, scattered around us, patches of lichen-like fungus do
glow in the dark. They are eerie when we turn our flashlights off,
but we try to go without light as much as possible just in case
someone approaches. Rob and I take turns daring to sit in our cold,

three-inch deep "pool." Mud is everywhere. We lean on each other while balancing on one foot to change into dry clothes without making them dirty. Just as we think we are getting the hang of it, a little mountain frog makes a loud sharp noise from a rock right in the middle of our private bath. We both leap up and land in a sprawling heap, spilling everything into the mud, including ourselves!

Everyone sleeps comfortably during the night through the rain, with one exception. The tree we have pitched our tarp under is laden with red fruits. Approximately every fifteen minutes one of these comes to its appointed hour. "Bong-ng-ng!"

When the morning sun beams into our camp bright with hope, I find myself with mixed feelings. No doubt I have chosen the right route. Max did well the day before, but he could not have gone any farther. If he went up the other ridge we would have run out of time. In fact we would have had to make camp on the trail completely short of cloud forest in a place where Wayne's previous party had been unable to find any fresh water.

But I am disappointed. My way has not produced my expected results, either. By my calculations, we should be well above the 900 meter level. Yet this is not the type of forest which we need to photograph at night. Very few mountain frogs cried out during the night, and I heard no audible bats. Some glow fungus litters the ground here and there but great patches didn't light up the night as in true cloud forest. What has gone wrong?

Max and Karl have lost confidence in me completely. They believe we headed in the wrong direction the day before and are now dallying aimlessly in the wilderness. I decide to let them stay in camp to rest and photograph the surrounding area. The rest of us get ready to go on ahead and clear the way to the top of Mount Hunstein. Soon I will know the whereabouts of cloud forest. I will be able to convince them to move higher up accordingly on the next day.

We do our chores. Water bottles are filled. We pack cheese, crackers and dried apricots along with the controversial map. Gogomo, Jim, Bahio, Rob and I set off up the trail at a leisurely pace.

Certainly this forest is different than the one at Gipa. Many more birds of paradise call out than below, though they remain hidden in the canopy. I am most thrilled to see hornbills.

These huge birds are so awkward in the air that you can hear their wings flapping what is thought to be up to a mile away. When they glide overhead, it sounds like a distant jet airplane landing. Hornbills compare in size with large eagles but have giant beaks. They wear penguin colors except that the males have golden heads. Frolicsome and curious, they clamber about in the tops of the largest fruit trees, making little grunting sounds.

When I was a child, we awoke every morning to the jet stream sound of hornbills. On family vacations, we looked forward to hearing their flights as soon as we crossed the ridge from Wagu. In recent years they have become quite rare. I am overjoyed to find them once again in the heart of Hunstein Forest.

A shy, endangered black palm cockatoo swoops in at one point and perches low on a branch where he can watch us with rare curiosity. His head tips from side to side and his giant crest rises and falls with his loud, dramatic, donkey-like cry. I can't identify another large red parrot and several flowers of different sorts. Neither I nor the Bahinemos have ever seen them. These give reason for our endeavor. These rare and beautiful plants and creatures must be preserved before they disappear from the earth.

The air is fresh and the atmosphere cheerful. We find ourselves feeling strong, well and playful. We pretend to claim huge, gangling, Swiss Family Robinson type trees as we pass them, specifying the rooms we would build if they were houses. I tell fables from Western tribal times in the Middle Ages. I tell them how our ancestors came to America and how modern civilization came about. They are especially interested in the history of the American Civil War, and of course in the tales which feature trolls, such as "Rumpelstiltskin" and "The Emperor's New Clothes".

Now and then, we peer down through the trees on one or the other of the sides of the ridge. In the far distance below us we see lively blues and greens graced with clouds. Shortly, we reach the place where Karl and Gogomo reported the "great chasm." This is the end of the known trail.

Gogomo cuts a vine as thick as a man's arm to stretch our water and we drink the light watery sap. It is sweet and refreshing. We eat half of the apricots. Thus fortified, we start down the mountain in the direction where the sun and the map tell me we should find a farther ridge. Sure enough, after a hundred-foot descent, we begin to go up again.

Now, Gogomo is cutting a new trail, and it is hard work. He wields his machete with wide sweeps, slashing vines and saplings up to two inches in diameter with each blow. I urge him not to make a "highway" and to conserve his energy, but he seems to feel we won't be going far enough to make him tired. We continue to rise higher and higher.

Abruptly the trail gets steeper. The distant sound of water from the valleys disappears. A cold mist surrounds us and the brush becomes thick as there are fewer trees to keep it in shade. We literally climb now, holding onto small saplings for support. Moss covers the forest floor at last. Could this be the actual top? Our hearts burst with anticipation. The outline of a knoll appears just above us surrounded by sky in all directions. Gogomo, who has been slowing down, renews his effort with great vigor. We can't help rushing to our goal and strain to overcome the steepness. Suddenly we are there. "Yay! This must be it!" We squeal, looking out at solid clouds in every direction. But Gogomo is skeptical.

The mist clears. Rising magnificently on the far side of a deep valley stands a mountain taller than this.

My father taught us that to survive in the rainforest we had to keep our heads together. Fears and opinions of others around you and even your own fears can lead you into trouble. To the dismay of the carriers, who believe this is the absolute end of the trail, I remain undaunted. By now my husband also wants to turn back, but I have my eyes squarely on the map.

Mt. Hunstein has a lump on the top of it, like a peak of cream on a hot fudge sundae. Perhaps the "taller mountain" is that peak.

The view is astounding. We can see all the way to Ambunti, where Rob's helper dropped the fuel barrel in the boat. The lake and the peninsula which we know hold Wagu village spread out before us. Mountain ridge after mountain ridge appear lower than we are. I decide this is the perfect opportunity to measure our directions and find out where we have been all this time. First I observe the direction of the sun, which, on the equator, is precisely West in the afternoon.

I lay out the map and over a delicious picnic, surrounded at last by true moss forest laden with tiny crimson orchids, we plot ridges and hills.

To the left, we can see that the ridge where the old camps lay is below us. I find them on the map and can tell from their altitude how far up the mountain we must be. The hills where Rob's plane landed, line up with the shore of the southern end of Wagu Lake. This gives us a true line of direction. With all this information I am able to draw an "X" on the map showing exactly where we are. According to this reading, the top of Mount Hunstein must indeed be that peak that is higher than us and we must be very close to it. I begin to consider how far the peak actually is from us. I can see palm trees and other trees with familiar sizes along its side. They appear large enough to be less than a kilometer away. This confirms the spot where I have just calculated us to be on the map. I figure we are almost there at last. It's time to move on.

"But San Edie," the men protest when they realize I am serious, "it's impossible. It would take three days at least, and it probably can't be done. We don't want to go." I look at them with shock and amazement. They're not tired. They have just hacked down a small tree with enthusiasm to gain a better view of the chasm before us and climbed another to collect the foot-long cocoon nest of a giant lunar moth, which they will use for cloth after eating the larva.

"Why are you telling me three days, when I showed you the exact place where we are on the map?" I ask them.

Then at last Gogomo levels with me. "Hasn't anyone told you that no one can ever go up on the true head of a mountain? When we were coming up the side of this knoll, even Jim thought this might be it, but he is young. We know that all mountains have several legs. These are the ridges. In the middle they have a head. The head is surrounded by a great chasm which goes way back down to sea-level. Can you not see this chasm spread out before us?" Gogomo points to the valley below. A distant roar of rushing rivers seems to billow up from its mysterious depths. I try not to picture a gigantic octopus.

"No one has ever gone across this barrier to the real head of the mountain. There is no doubt we have now gone as far as anyone can go, and the real head is indeed what you see right across there."

"But our family went to the top when I was a kid," I argue.

"That's what you have always thought," Gogomo replies. "We never had the heart to tell your family the truth. Of course your guides never took you to the real top of the mountain. They brought you as far as a point such as this. It was surrounded by clouds, and your family thought it was the top. It was late at the time, and the men knew if you didn't turn back, you would never get back up the walls of the chasm in time to return to your camp, so they told you that you had reached the end of the route. No one argued with them. They didn't lie to you; they just didn't have the heart to tell you the whole truth. No one has ever been up on the real mountain head."

My own head is spinning. There is no use trying to convince the carriers the top is even reachable let alone vulnerable to loggers. I am amazed and devastated. No wonder they have been hiking so slowly. I have the feeling we might have even made it by now if we had started out at a reasonable hour and lingered less. But it's only 1:30 PM. We still have plenty of time to explore before returning to camp.

"I want to try," I tell them. They looked worried. Gogomo looks hurt. "Look," I say, "What harm can be done if we travel just one hour further? We can easily get back to camp after that and you will then know if the map is true or the old stories. Jim, you can take over the cutting and Gogomo can take a break for a while. He has been cutting such a wide trail that you haven't had to cut at all up 'till now."

"Agreed," they reply, after some deliberation. "One hour is all you will get, and then we go back. Which way do you propose to head?" they ask a touch sarcastically.

I would cut the trail myself if I could wield a machete with any kind of skill. We need a trail cut in case Max and Karl want to follow the next day. Rob pulls me aside and gives me one of those looks which people who are married get on occasion and would rather forget."Are you sure you're not on some personal vendetta?" he exclaims. "You've got to be crazy." By now, maybe I am. I am no longer thinking about the goal of cloud forest and am obsessed with reaching the summit.

We go no further than sixty feet in the direction I choose based on the map before it becomes clear that a narrow and easily traversable ridge extends as neatly as a bridge between our peak and the next. We are heading up, not down into a chasm.

Abruptly a massive section of trees thrown down by a storm blocks us. An unrelenting sun permeates the area around these fallen logs, which are jammed to heights far above our heads. Around them, flourishing in the light of the now open canopy, is a thick tangled jumble of vines and brush. These form a solid barricade which we cannot penetrate. Everyone stops. Tropical flowers and the steady hum of insects grace the air. At this obstacle, I am sure the men will give up but they work all the harder, checking their watches for the agreed upon time. Jim cuts a tunnel straight into the tangle of vegetation on the right, but after twenty feet of carving, he has not broken through. Meanwhile, Gogomo seems to be making some headway to the left, and we follow him.

Suddenly Rob lets out a blood-curdling scream. He throws himself on the ground and writhes in pain; his face contorted in agony. Clutching his chest he moans. I throw myself on the ground next to him wondering what on earth is happening. I stare into the tunnel. Gogomo rushes out of it yelling, "Bees, bees!"

Three large welts rise on Rob's chest. They have red holes in the center of them. I don't see any stingers, but the area around the wounds is swelling fast. We have to wait on the ground for ten minutes before the bees settle in the hive and it is safe to stand up. I worry about Rob going into shock but he seems alert so I urge all of us into Jim's tunnel which he has at last managed to cut through the debris on the right.

Trying to prove a point, or perhaps eager to see if I am right, the carriers rush on ahead. There are fifteen minutes left in my promised hour. Soon they are out of sight and out of earshot. Rob and I lag behind. After ten more minutes, Rob begins to get angry. In addition to the pain, he is becoming nauseated. These are apparently no ordinary bees. He has had enough and wants to return to camp immediately.

It seems wise to stay with the Bahinemos, however, in case anything happens. I cannot carry Rob. I urge Rob to press on toward them, but he begins to stumble and mutter to himself. He sits down and refuses to go any farther. Maybe he is going into shock! I beg him to stay in one spot and then run on up the trail to get the others.

A few yards ahead, I find Bahio sitting on a high log from which she can see straight up a massive incline. "It is the real head!"

The men are gone, exhilarated that they indeed crossed the great chasm.

"They're going up!" she exclaims with girlish excitement when she sees me. "They say this is really it. You were right. We made it."

The men are too far off to call.

"I have to turn back," I say. Disappointment is noticeable on my face and in my voice. "Tell the men Rob is not doing well. I'm taking him back to camp."

I run back down the trail, trying to remember how far back I left him. At last I come to the spot where he sat down. He is gone. I look around and call his name. There is no answer.

He wasn't thinking straight. He must have tried to go back alone. A horrible thought fills my mind. What if he got disoriented and wandered over the side of the ridge? As much as he loves the rainforest, Rob was raised in the city. He would never get far following the trail even if he wasn't being overcome by the bees. And what sort of bees are these? Does anyone know what their venom might do? We are way beyond territory known biologically by either scientists or Bahinemos. These bees might be capable of anything. I run on, frantic, calling his name every few minutes.

The farther I go, the more the trail's distance seems to multiply. I see different kinds of trees, gullies, tussocks and hollows that I don't remember and would give in to sheer panic if not for the occasional ones that I do recall, and a few telling slash marks from machetes. How far back are the bees? Shouldn't we have passed them by now? What if Rob missed the tunnel and walked right back into the hive?

Rob is sitting on a log by the side of the trail. He went as far as where he thought the bees might be and waited for the rest of us to return. The distance I just ran was only my adrenaline induced imagination. His pain is at last beginning to subside.

Gogomo and Jim appear in a short time, followed by Bahio. Bahio shrieks and throws herself to the side of the trail. "Snake!" she cries. She is only a few feet from where Rob has been sitting. Jim runs to her rescue pulling out his machete and then stops and begins to laugh. "What!" She glares at her husband indignantly. We rush to her side. It's a brilliant, green tree python, the so-called "shy snake" prized as pets the world over. The biggest mystery is that he is still asleep, wrapped around a small sapling which Gogomo cut on his way up and threw across the trail. Each of us stepped over it on the way, and again on the way back without seeing it. How much more are we missing?

Rob is the only one brave enough to pick up the small sapling with the snake wrapped around it to take back to Max for photos. When at last the snake awakens, I put a forked stick over its neck and Rob picks it up. This rejuvenates Rob and there is great merriment and joking as we make our way back, careful not to get too close to the snake which is coiled in a knot around Rob's arm.

It's only an hour and a half back to camp.

When we arrive we are startled to find Max securely stationed in his bed with eyes wide open, alert. He too was stung by bees. When he returned to camp, he looked down to find his sock filled to overflowing with blood. A careful search reveals a leech as round and full as a marble and a 1/4 inch round "hole" in his left ankle. Leeches possess a powerful anti-coagulant which can cause even surface bites to bleed profusely, often before their victims feel their presence. Those of us with bare feet are able to avoid this hazard by quickly checking our feet whenever we feel something sticky. Max had not been expecting anything to crawl into his socks, and I forgot to warn him.

On hearing this, Gogomo sets about collecting many saplings, vines and some bark, and cleverly fashions an American style sofa for Max to rest on. Several harmless types of bees are flying around the camp, however, so Max doesn't use the sofa but remains in his netted bed until dusk drives them away.

I had left a bag of beans soaking in a pot all day. By dusk they are soft enough to add rice and a can of hot dogs. This meal restores us. Much to the dismay of Max and Karl, I demand that on the following day they should both walk at least as far as the mossy peak. In addition I have asked that they consider going farther, hiking a total of three more hours to match the original distance Max had agreed to in Washington D.C. when we all still thought we would be using the old, steep route. I am certain there will be even better mossy places to photograph farther up the trail. Wouldn't it be nice, I think, if we could bring pictures of the actual mountain top back to the magazine in addition to the various types of rainforest?

Karl still does not believe we are even on the right slope and is ready to take Max back to Gipa. Max's insect injuries are routine, and I don't think they would excuse him should I later be asked why he did not hike at least as far as he planned. The three hours I am asking Max and Karl for might even take them clear to the top. Max, Karl and Rob go directly to bed.

I stir up the coals and adjust the canvas pack I am sitting on to bring myself closer to the fire. It's been a satisfying day, but we haven't accomplished our goals. Tomorrow is Sunday; our last chance to photograph cloud forest before supplies are gone.

Jim mumbles something in his wife's language, which I don't understand. Jim speaks a little of her Kagiru, but Gogomo knows it well as he was also born into that neighboring tribe before he was adopted by the Bahinemos as a child. Whatever Gogomo says in response to Jim's comments makes Bahio smirk. Then she looks serious. I can hear sarcasm in their voices and ask them what they are saying. Embarrassed, Jim says, "Nothing really." A thin trail of smoke rises from the dying fire. Somewhere in the dark a strange clicking sound indicates an insect or a frog.

"Listen guys," I say. "You'd be surprised what I understand. Sometimes you see me act in a Western way, but that's because I have a job to do in the Western world. I can't make everybody happy at once. Every conflict in the group splits my heart between the

Western way of thinking and the Bahinemo way. Tell me what you're talking about."

They look at each other for a few moments, and then Gogomo responds. While he talks, he digs his toes nervously into the soft leaves and dirt.

"There are several things we don't understand: First, it's wrong to work on Sunday and yet you are asking us to go back to the mountain top tomorrow. We also want to go, but it will require more work in one day than we have done on this whole trip so far. As a Christian, how can you justify this? When we have non-Christian bosses we walk off the job on Sundays unless they give us at least double pay. Sometimes we leave anyway!"

The question has been inevitable. Doubling their pay is not a problem, but I need to respect their religious beliefs. After what happened the week before, I know full well the situation calls for much more than a simple bribe. For the moment, I assure them that I understand their convictions. I tell them I am also conflicted, but that I am responsible to *National Geographic* to carry out their mission. I remind them the magazine spent thousands of dollars to get us here and that tomorrow is the only day in history that our work can be accomplished. I say that I personally think God would accept this, and ask them to think about the matter some more during the night and give me their decision in the morning. I won't force them to go against their consciences.

This leads to problem number two:

"We understand quite well that the way of the outside world is that the top person gets hundreds of dollars per day, the next one down gets tens of dollars per day, and the workers at the bottom, like us, get next to nothing even though they usually work the hardest. We have come to accept this. But you are one of us. You must know better. Why do you also operate in this heathen manner?" asks Jim.

It's time to take a deep breath. I say a prayer for wisdom and do some fast thinking. I struggled with this question for years, especially when I first moved to the United States. I begin by telling them this and that there are no easy answers.

Then I explain that it would be a significant disruption for me to do things in any different way. Government representatives asked that we not pay carriers more than the minimum standard wage as doing so would make it impossible for them to carry out research expeditions with their own much lower budgets. We Westerners , meanwhile, need a much higher wage, lest we lose our house, our electricity and food back in the U.S. "I wouldn't be able to find trees to build a new house in Dallas," I assure them. "And there is no place for Rob and me to plant an adequate garden if we run out of money for food."

"But why can't you pay just *us* a high wage?" they want to know. "We'll understand this is an exception. We won't demand more from government expeditions after this, and we won't even tell the rest of the village."

Some Westerners encountering these types of situations declare their third world workers to be rebellious or "backward thinking". The Bahinemos are as intellectual and courteous as my Western friends, perhaps more so. However they are grappling with the beginnings of capitalism.

I agree to pay just these three more money per day while they are away from the rest of the group up on the mountain. I don't have to do this, but in choosing to, I convince them I care for them and respect their views. They in turn promise to work the next day, "only for me as family." This isn't about business. It's about relationships. I am doing it their way. There is a new, deep bond between us much like the one I developed on the previous expedition with Ma Lekim. From now on we walk as equals; partners in a quest. The imperialistic aura is gone and we are, at last, real colleagues.

And I am finally able to communicate with some Bahinemos.

At night I sleep soundly despite the fruit bombs.

In the morning the carriers want a devotional. I decide to hold an optional service after breakfast, which all attend except Max and Karl. Gogomo asks me to read passages from the Bible about the Sabbath. I can see they still don't feel at peace about the issue.

After I translate the Ten Commandments, I turn to the New Testament where Jesus was accused and persecuted for healing on the Sabbath. He responded by reminding the temple priests that even they would rescue a lost sheep on that day.

When I get to this part, Jim's face forms a wide grin. "Let's go!" he shouts, raising his fists with enthusiasm. Gogomo agrees and Bahio, giggling at her husband's fervor, also smiles and nods in agreement. Everyone decides to end the service with a quick prayer and to leave immediately.

160

New route view of scientists' camps

Orchids

Chapter 17

On the Forehead of the Mountain

*~~ On cool lazy mornings I would lie
in my dug-out canoe and stare at the top of
Mount Hunstein reflected in the water among
the lilies.~~*

Karl and Max agree to go directly to the moss peak and
decide from there whether or not to pursue my requested three hours
of hiking. I hope they will go farther but they have no intention of
going to the top, which is fine, since their real goal is to photograph
cloud forest. Gogomo and Jim plan to forge ahead of the rest of us,
cutting a trail on up the final peak. Bahio and I will take turns
carrying the lunch, the tripod and Max's smallest camera bag as far
as Max and Karl feel they can make it. Then we will leave these
things with them and proceed up the trail the men cut. At whatever
point they stop, Karl and Max are supposed to work their way back
to camp alone with their own equipment taking pictures as they go.
Rob opts to stay in camp by himself and finish his novel. He doesn't
want to risk the bees again.

At first Karl and Max stop every few minutes. They keep
finding interesting plants and wanting to take pictures. Karl finds a
strange purple flower which he declares is an undiscovered form of
tomato. He is thrilled. The entire trip is now worth it, he announces.
The ultimate purpose of our trip is to save such species. Max takes
lots of pictures of the flower while the rest of us sit and wait.

We make whistles out of a tall thin grass. We bat harmless
black ants off of our legs, wrinkling our noses at the smell of
formaldehyde they give off. I long for a pair of shorts rather than my
culottes so I can climb a tree that angles way up to a magnificent
view. Finally, when they finish with that specimen, I announce that
other pictures must be taken on the way back. Max and Karl aren't
hurrying. They don't believe we are actually heading anywhere. It's
almost as late as it was when we reached this far the day before.

We arrive at the mossy point after an easy forty-five minute walk from camp. Max agrees to continue on until 1:45 PM. That should give him 2 hours to get back and 2 hours to photograph on the way before dark. Shortly we pass the limit of yesterday's adventures, being careful to use Jim's tunnel on the right where the bees do not live. Everyone is together as we begin to ascend the actual high rounded peak of Mount Hunstein.

The forest has moss but only a little. The trees are small on the ridge where storm winds have blown many of them down. This means the sun gets through, making it drier and causing more bamboo to grow than what I remember from the ridge of the previous year. We keep hoping for real cloud forest. I begin to realize our route has taken us up the drier side of the mountain. We might never find what I remember.

1:45 arrives and it is time for Max to turn back. I lay down his gear for him as planned and hand him some extra snacks and a poncho in case of bad weather.

Suddenly Karl drops his gear, grabs his machete, and runs ahead. "Here! I'm going up to the top and YOU can baby-sit Max!" He shouts in Tok Pisin, undecipherable to Max.

We are stunned. He hasn't even believed me that there is a mountain top in this direction until now. If it wasn't for *his* negative attitude about how far Max could make it, we might have been able to hike far more efficiently and be much farther along. Instead, we have tried to be patient as both Karl and Max dawdled, complaining incessantly. All the while we hoped we could make up for the time as soon as they turned back.

There is no way I can leave Max alone without Karl. One of us has to return to camp with him.

Fortunately Karl's professional side comes to the rescue. After a few minutes he comes bounding back, shouting for Max to come up the trail just ten minutes farther. He has found real moss forest!

The moss casts a light green glow over all of the roots, hollows, branches and trees around us. It isn't as thick as I would like, but it is beautiful. Max sets up his tripod and looks at angles while Karl identifies plants. I say good-bye and wish them luck, laying the camera bag on the ground next to Max.

Karl is furious.

"I'm not going to carry that camera bag all the way back to camp," he declares. "That's what we hired carriers for." Everyone looks at Bahio, the only carrier present. Her eyes are full of fear. Her husband would never leave her to return to camp alone with two men. She looked forward to the journey to the top of the mountain even when her husband was skeptical about it. Jim is near but I need him to help clear the trail. Besides, I had given them my word, "no extra work on Sunday," and they had given me theirs, "We'll go up for you alone." Karl agreed that morning to remain with Max no matter what. He will have to accept it.

Bahio and I run up the trail and leave the men fuming. We catch up to Jim and ask him what to do. He is angry when he hears what just happened. "If the young men were here instead of us, like Karl and Max wanted, they would have attacked Karl for acting like this," he says. "They had better be glad you chose us older men."

"Still, I can't just walk away and leave them," I say.

Reaching the top of Mount Hunstein isn't required by the *National Geographic*. We have only been asked to photograph cloud forest. But we are so close. I desperately want to go on.

"Come on, San Edie. Let's catch up with Ma Gogomo and see what he says." Jim replies. "He is wise and will help us decide whether we should go back or continue on. We can't leave Gogomo alone on the mountain without even telling him we're turning back, and I'm sure not going to leave my wife alone with those men."

My first responsibility is to Max but I know he's safe with Karl. Neither he nor Karl are tired and camp is only two hours away. As a PNG scientist, Karl should know the forest better than anybody. They just don't like the idea of carrying their own gear. I begin to realize that deep in his heart, most of Karl's griping might have been "sour grapes". He is in far better shape than I am and probably resents having to tag along with a photographer when he would love to be exploring. After all, this is part of his country. We proceed after Gogomo.

But Gogomo is gone!

Right after we leave Karl and Max we come to a place where a beautiful rushing stream crashes down off of the side of the mountain through great hollows of moss, boulders and trees. It's gorgeous; what a place for a camp.

However, we don't stop even for a minute because we have to find Gogomo. We climb faster and faster and every few feet one of us calls out. We are not using a Western type call which would penetrate only a few yards of forest, but rather, the shrill high-pitched yodel of the Bahinemo that can be heard for up to a mile if the terrain is right. Still there is no answer.

Up and up we go. The trail disappears and all that is left to tell us Gogomo is somewhere ahead is a very occasional machete slash mark or broken branch. Obviously he stopped making a trail at some point and is "running like a pig" as the Bahinemos say.

At one point, Jim also disappears, leaving us women behind. Bahio's face is clenched tight, a mixture of fear and courage. She tells me all she can think of are the mountain trolls. Have the same ones that took Gogomo away now taken her husband? She expects us to be ambushed any minute. Finally we catch up to Jim and she stays very close to him.

We keep on coming to places where the sky surrounds a knoll above and ahead of us and think that it's the top. Each time, the mountain leads us on to another rise. On and up we go, seemingly forever. Bamboo and trees become a blur. Arms and legs alternately grow stiff as they try to adapt to climbing vertically from sapling to sapling.

Sometimes Jim and Bahio wait while I catch up. Other times I get ahead and have to wait for them. Once we can't find Gogomo's trail at all and consider turning back. Then I discover a broken twig far to the left of where we have been heading. He had come to a huge boulder and maneuvered around it. Or was the twig broken by an animal? We follow it.

We are now deep in cloud and wonder what view there would be if we could see. The terrain begins to lose its steepness at last. That is, on the average it seems to proceed horizontally forward. In fact, it goes up and down like a zigzag turned sideways with thirty foot crevasses everywhere. It's more difficult to navigate than ever.

To our astonishment, we come to a place where a human has gouged a chunk out of a tree about a year before judging by the new layer of moss growing in it. It must have been Dr. Allison. Allen Allison, a lead scientist on the previous expedition, claimed to have reached the summit of Mt. Hunstein the year before, along with his PNG carrier. Our trail has apparently joined up with theirs from the old camp on the South ridge. He talked about a false peak. Is this it? Or did he come this far and mark it, thinking this was the real summit?

Still there is no Gogomo.

We go on crossing many steep dips and rises where thousands of feet fall away on either side. I know we have reached the whipped cream shaped peak, but I want to get to the highest point. After so much confusion, I want to confirm our conquest by actually viewing the valley on the opposite side. It is 4:00 PM.

Suddenly there is a cry of joy. Bahio hears Gogomo yodeling close by. We hurry on, having to cross a rather large crevasse filled with deep moss in order to follow the sound. There on a high point on the other side of the crevasse sits Gogomo, gesturing wildly. He is very happy to see us.

"Come up. Come up. San Edie, we're here!" he yells. "Look, we have conquered the head of the mountain," He is overjoyed.

I look across through branches and can see the outline of a hill full of trees about twenty minutes away. It's higher than we are. This is not the top.

"But you don't understand. San Edie, listen to me," Gogomo shouts in triumph. He breaks into my reverie. "We HAVE made it to the top!"

Gogomo is exasperated, "You know what's wrong with you white people?" he says, "You're never satisfied with just getting on top of the head of a mountain, you think you have to get to the tip of the crown. You tell your boss that you went all the way to the forehead! You tell her in our country it makes no difference whether something sits on your forehead or your crown. It is still the top of your head. You tell her that. We made it to the top. That spot over there is nothing. We have to go home now. It will be a miracle if we get there by dark, and we have no flashlights."

I burst out laughing. We all laugh hysterically, picturing ourselves on the forehead of some big giant. Part of me laughs. Part of me cries.

Of course Gogomo is right. There is no way we can go even those twenty minutes farther. He did go half-way there, he says, but turned back thinking that if I never made it behind him he would steal the glory of my trip. "Nonsense," I say. "You should have done it yourself and turned back for us. Somebody should have made it."

It's almost poetic that the mountain has conquered us again. Perhaps no one has ever made it to the real summit, in spite of the claims. Perhaps the Bahinemo people are right.

Bahio lets out a terrible scream, breaking the silence. She comes crashing back to us from several yards away. She had been leaning over and peering into the clouds from a tree stump when the clouds cleared suddenly, producing a view thousands of feet directly below her. Even the helicopter didn't take her that high above the earth.

The view from the mountain is incredible. I am amazed that such an isolated place can still exist in today's world, and that I am fortunate enough to experience it. Mount Hunstein represents the whole Hunstein Region and the importance of preserving it.

I take a few photos of the silhouette of the "real" crest with my little disposable camera, and we drink and eat our last water and food. We have an hour and a half to get back to camp.

Down we go, leaping from sapling trunk to sapling trunk. I brought a pair of shoes this time, and am glad I did. Even the Bahinemos wish they had shoes. Their feet are no match for the bamboo shards scattered everywhere.

We fill our canteens when we reach the beautiful moss laden stream and waterfall which Karl and Max just missed seeing. We drink deeply, tossing water on our arms and faces. I long to stay.

We rush on, past the tunnel past the bee tree, over the mossy peak where the men had reported the great chasm. My arms and legs go numb. The trail before me seems to swim. I reach a point where I feel I cannot take another step.

It's getting dark fast, so I urge Gogomo to go on ahead and get flashlights lest we become stranded, but he refuses to leave us. I know Karl would never be able to search for us alone. Mentally I imagine the four of us huddled in some hollow in a pouring night rain.

Meanwhile, I pull each leg forward over and over, swinging heavily on my walking stick. My face must show the strain because Jim and Gogomo begin to reassure me every few feet. "You're going to make it, San Edie," they say with deep gentleness and concern. "Come on, just a little bit farther."

The trail is a mess. Max and Karl must have had a terrible time, because there are skid marks all the way down from the moss peak. I fall twice in their skids.

Just as the trail becomes invisible in the dark, we stumble into camp.

Chapter 18

Poison

*~~ My dad ate the lemon fruit. It was called
"yi". He got very sick, swelled up all over and was
very quiet. We had to take him out of the forest and a
long ways down river to a doctor.~~*

I anticipate that Rob would have found it rough being alone
in the forest for a whole day. I expect him to be stressed and worried
sick about us being gone until dark. Instead his angry words when
we arrive in camp are, "What in the world did you do to get Karl and
Max so mad?"

I am much too exhausted to respond. Someone stokes the fire
and quickly heats supper. Everyone eats in silence. I struggle to the
dark, muddy creek alone to rinse off. Rob is completely
unsupportive. Even when I crawl into our tent, I am too tired to
explain to him anything that happened. "Did you make it to the
top?" he asks me.

"Nope," I reply.

We are hurt by each other's behavior. Still, I am satisfied.
Max got all the pictures he needed and I made it up the mountain.

As we start to doze off, a terrible storm rises up out of
nowhere. Thunder and lightning rail and flash, but far worse than
that, we hear trees falling all around us. Suddenly large branches are
falling down on our camp. Something crashes with a dreadful
tearing noise on the tarp over our tents. Bahio and I scream. Karl
and Rob run hysterically about the camp, looking vainly for
something for us all to hide under. Gogomo prays loudly. Wind
shrieks through the camp and hundreds of the little fruits pound
above our heads as though the entire forest is falling. As suddenly as
it began, everything is quiet. A quick check reveals no damage.

Monday morning I wake up and begin to itch. My world takes on a surreal distant feel and I wonder if all the pressure has been too much.

Before breakfast Rob and I go for a walk to talk out our differences. He hadn't realized the carriers and I had had an ordeal. He's still too naive about matters in the rainforest to know that if a party hasn't returned before dusk, something serious must have happened. Rob tells me Max and Karl had staggered into camp only moments before us. I never learn why. Apparently, just before we arrived, they told their side of the argument about carrying the gear. This left Rob with the impression that they had had an even harder time than we who had stumbled in silently.

At least our photo requirements on the mountain have been done to the best of our ability though we never did find the true drizzling wet cloud forest. We can go back down now. There are other places that need to be photographed down river from Gipa.

"You don't look too good," Rob says to me gently, on our way back to camp when we have talked all this out. "I won't have you carrying a pack on the way down. Something is wrong."

We pack up camp and the supplies are divided out. Fortunately for me, having eaten our food, we are one pack lighter. I feel like I am drugged as I start down the trail, walking stick tightly in hand.

We haven't gone far when the carriers from Gipa meet us on their way up. They take up the loads we left for them in camp and all of us proceed down in a great line.

Each time we stop to catch our breath and drink, I fall asleep on the damp ground. My eyes swell to slits.

Wamseli and his wife are excited about the enormous dog tracks they saw on the way down when we came up. " The tracks were right by the fire that your group built," they say.

"*Us*," we all exclaim. "We thought *your* group built the fire." Was this the fire and the dog of the renegade Japanese man, we wonder? By the time we get to the spot with the ashes, only one track is left and it is no longer clear, leaving it all a mystery.

Bahio declares when she walks past the lake that if she ever comes here again she will place baby crocodiles in it. "What a deal," she exclaims. "Why, a few years later I could come back and find them still confined there, big and fat and ready to harvest."

The only way to cross the river at the bottom of the ridge is to walk down a giant log. Below me the water appears a raging torrent. As I approach the shore on the other side, the ground also sways. A few minutes later I stagger in circles, wondering how to get my balance. After that I lean on Rob until we make it to Gipa, where Ma Lekim rushes to greet us. I can only stutter terribly and retreat into our tent which Rob hastily puts up.

In the tent, I discover that patches of a poison ivy like rash cover me from head to toe. By this time I can barely see through my swollen eyes. Obviously, this is some sort of allergic reaction. Much to my relief I am sick, not crazy.

I am too disoriented at first to connect the reaction to a sweet smelling fruit which I had foolishly taken a tiny taste of up on the mountain the morning before. Karl had identified the family of the tree it was found on, and assured me that it should be safe to try, though he did not attempt this himself. I come to believe the tempting fruit is probably the cause of my malaise. I scrounge up a good dose of Benadryl and Moyali makes dinner for the camp.

Chapter 19

Rivers to Cross

~~ Darkness was on its way. We had a late start that morning. We had more to pack than usual because our family wanted to camp by ourselves. Maybe we just wanted to see if we could do it. It was raining and the river was in flood. Mom set up the camp while my two brothers and Dad built a crude shelter. We could skimp on the frame and rely on our tarpaulins, but we couldn't skimp on the fireplace.

Mom wanted the fireplace to be up off of the ground and made of clay like always. She wouldn't tolerate smoke from the moldy ground coming into our shelter or bending her knees in the mud to stoke the fire. My younger sister and I, twelve and thirteen, were sent to get clay. The only clay we knew of was on an island. Carefully we leaned against the power and fury of the current as we crossed the raging river on a submerged log holding our hands and the empty bucket. Then we had to get back across with it full of clay. ~~

We start downriver toward Bani early the next day. It will be our last camp in the rainforest before we hike out to Wagu.

Ma Lekim feels much better. He insists on carrying a camera case for Max. Ma Lekim has washed our clothes and kept the whole camp in shape while we were gone. Although we have used up most of the food there is far more equipment than our nine carriers can carry. Most of them will have to return to Gipa for second loads the next day, while Karl and Max are photographing Bani. The walk from Gipa to Bani is longer and more tedious than any we have undertaken so far, but no one seems to complain.

Max doesn't say anything about his struggle up on the mountain. Nor does he say a word about our frivolous ambition to reach the top. He doesn't even mention whether he got pictures of cloud forest. In fact, he seems to have forgotten all of it. He is cheerful about heading toward civilization and not the least bit afraid of the hike, even though we warn him it will involve crossing the river many times. He actually shows me quite a bit of concern, wishing I could get to a doctor. My head has cleared during the night and my eyes are open just enough so I can see. I am still somewhat weak and the red blisters I am covered with are excruciatingly itchy. Nevertheless, there is nothing for me to do but go on.

At this point the purpose of our expedition eludes me and I can only think of survival.

I lag behind on the trail, and feel sorry for Jim and Bahio, who insist on waiting for me. Their massive loads would be far easier to carry at their own pace. We plod along as fast as I can manage.

Max stays well ahead of us even when we must wade through knee deep mud, cross slippery rapids, and squirm around thorns. Either he has finally gotten the hang of it all, or he is simply resigned to his fate. I'm sure the fact we are heading toward civilization helps.

We hear a sudden terrible ruckus up ahead with lots of shouting, yelling and squeals. We rush through mud and water to our shins to where Karl, Max, Moyali and Mathew gather in a huddle. The tiniest, cutest, twin baby cassowaries I have ever seen nestle in Karl and Moyali's arms. Having startled the family, Karl and Moyali boldly and recklessly threw themselves on the young chicks before the mother realized what happened. She quickly disappeared into the forest before we got there.

Karl beams. "I've always wanted a baby cassowary," he exclaims. "The last thing my boys said to me before I left was, 'Bring me back a baby cassowary, Daddy.'"

The gangly ten-inch chicks are covered with coarse, hairy down in gold and brown stripes. Karl talks in soothing whispers to his little creature. The baby's head bears no sign of the large, green helmet it will someday sprout. "Whirrr, whirrr" is its loud forlorn whistle. I am carrying our lunch over my shoulder in a small string bilum bag borrowed from Jim. With his permission, I empty the bag out and hand it to Karl so he can lock the baby inside. Moyali puts her baby bird in her own string bag. Meanwhile, Bahio looks with jealousy over our shoulders. She too, has always wanted a little cassowary.

Flood plain forest has a whole different flavor than the forests we left behind us. The trees are tall and majestic, holding the canopy far above like the roof of some gothic cathedral. Buttress roots create thin triangular support walls up to ten feet high and spreading ten feet out in every direction, making the tree bases twenty feet in diameter. Every now and then giant leaves, yellow with age, float gracefully down and down, swaying gently from side to side as they fall.

The forest floor is flat and covered with soft, damp mud. We are at an altitude where it floods only after large rains, not for whole months. There are many areas where the leaves on the ground are washed away. In such places the thin layer of flat mud records the tracks of whatever forest creatures happen along.

The vegetation is lush, only where the sun shines to the ground. The openings above the river and where the canopy has been breached due to fallen trees are bright places. In the dim twilight under the canopy, there is little undergrowth. Most greenery has dark broad leaves and looks like giant house plants. Whenever possible, we traverse the patches of thick brush around fallen trees by walking on the logs themselves. Only when a log has fallen diagonally across our path, or fallen so long ago it has almost disintegrated, do we find we must wriggle through the kind of thick vegetation and vines folklore attributes to "jungles".

At such times, and whenever else the light breaks through, such as near a river or a creek, it pays to keep a close eye out both on the ground and at eye level for nasty "Wait-A-Minute" vines. These vines are long stems covered with fishing hook-like thorns. These have a tendency to swing out over the trail just as you are passing by, especially if they are pushed aside by the person ahead. By grabbing a hold of your pack and yanking you to a stop, they effectively say, "Wait a minute!" If they snag your skin: Ouch!

The mountain is behind us, but we have a long way to go. Wagu and the lake at the edge of the rainforest are another whole day's hike away after this one. Our goals begin to come back to me as the day goes by and my health improves. Max needs to photograph this seasonal flood forest at Bani. Once we reach Wagu there is more work to do. Our editors have suggested that a few more photos of sago processing might be nice. In addition, there is another kind of rainforest for Max to photograph. The forest at the mouth of the Hunstein River floods for six months at a time. We must reach that forest at the other end of Wagu Lake by boat.

It starts to rain about halfway through our long trek to Bani. Besides getting wet, this means we have to keep a very close eye out for leeches. Leeches love to cling to wet leaves and can easily brush onto passersby. They are no problem if you flick them off before they have a chance to eat into your skin. At least there are no dangerous muddy slopes. The paths are slippery and the river is becoming deeper and faster.

By the time we get to the last place where we have to cross the river, its turbulent current flows chest high. For a few confusing minutes people wander up and down the bank until it is clear we have no choice but to go through it. Several men jump in, and after some deliberation, they determine a "shallowest" place. One by one we pass the men our loads and swim across.

The bank on the far side of the river is another one of the places where the forestry department camped on the expedition. Like Gipa, they cleared it of trees, leaving it covered with bug filled grass. However, it's the only site which is relatively safe from flooding in this area. There is one old rickety wood frame for a shelter which has a few bark racks that lay rotting on the ground.

We place the gear on these and cover it with a tarp to protect it from the continuing rain. It's no use getting dry clothes out of our packs. They would just get wet again.

As soon as we arrive, the carriers try to determine shelter sites. They are worried about flooding, and about the deep, bug filled grass on the high bank. They are worried about the sun that could heat up the tarps during the day and about whether the trees, which had been de-stabilized by the earlier cutting, might fall on the camp. They are also concerned about having to build a special, separate shelter for us outsiders.

"Just put us all under one roof," I tell them, eliminating the biggest problem they face. The rain continues to pour down on our unsheltered bodies. "I have never been happy with the way outsiders always seem to want to sleep separate from you," I tell the carriers. At this point I am unable to think of any reason why this is the way it's usually done. The Bahinemos are very relieved and begin to build a large tarp frame on the edge of the clearing near a stream where water can be drawn, but still on the high bank.

Rob, Max and I sit dismally. We don't know what to do to help. Stuck here in the rainforest, longing for a hot meal, warm bath and dry sheets, it's hard to remember that civilization is the ultimate enemy of this whole project.

Occasionally I wander over to watch the men cut saplings or the women tie them together with vines, and offer to lend a hand. Each time they deny my help. I don't know whether this is because I still do not look well, or just because under such urgent, hectic circumstances it would be more work to explain to me what to do than to just do it themselves. Certainly the Bahinemo women are having a terrible time doing their part. All shelter building is normally allocated to men.

In time, the bedraggled building crew works slower and slower. They become discouraged. The women place poles in awkward ways that probably won't hold. Each time the men return from the forest with supplies, they have to stop and re-do much of what the women have done. The men then explain to their wives once again, in exasperated tones, how the poles are supposed to be laid or tied. I finally get to help when they see that I am learning from these repeated instructions. Night falls very fast in the tropics. In rain it falls even faster. It is almost dark.

Realizing the gravity of the situation, Gogomo musters all of his powerful adrenaline and begins to huff and stomp about the camp with a great amount of gusto. He slashes his machete into small logs, chopping them in half, and flies from activity to activity, letting out loud karate like grunts and admonishing everyone to "step to it!" This startling enthusiasm gets everyone laughing. It's a great motivator.

Soon the frame is finished. We draw the tarps over it to create a shelter of thirty by twenty feet. Out of the rain at last!

It's so dark I can barely see, but I know I can't ask Rob or Max to sleep on the ground near all those bugs, which include chiggers. I don't relish adding such bites to my rash, either. I swallow hard and tell Jim and Gogomo we need to build beds. Jim looks like he is going to cry. They would normally have built platforms even for themselves at such a bug ridden site, but how can they get the materials needed before pitch dark?

With a lot of work, Gogomo had made Max's jungle hammock into a cot up on the mountain. He did this by threading long, straight saplings down through the seams on each side of the canvas bed. The two side poles had to be secured tightly to a firmly standing frame at each end or they would slide together. There is very little time, but at least such a bed doesn't require the bark covering of a real platform. Gogomo rushes back into the darkening forest to cut saplings and vines to build such a cot.

Jim and I look around and decide we can salvage the rotting bark which the supplies are resting on for a bed for Rob and I. Jim rushes into the forest for the materials to build our frame. Meanwhile, Bahio and Rob put together the tents.

When the roof is up, Moyali and Yamu turn their efforts toward building a fire. This is a challenge even with their skills, because the wood is soaked. But so are we, and in the dark we are beginning to get cold. Rain is still pouring down, so they place the fire just under the edge of the roof in the farthest corner from the beds. Soon smoke is billowing across the entire shelter.

Perhaps this is the sort of experience which makes some outsiders and even nationals forget why the rain forest is so important to save. Maybe misery like this is the reason so many people want to cut it down and clear it away for living space, even where there is no logging. A rainforest can be a temperamental kind of friend.

Max is cold and still wet. Bugs are beginning to crawl out of their resting places in droves. Everyone has been too busy to interpret for him, so he has no idea what severe challenges the carriers have faced in trying to get us shelter at all. He only knows they took an awfully long time and seem to have spent a lot of it just wandering around talking. Even though a roof is up now, no separate shelter has been built for him and there is nowhere to change into dry clothes. The whole purpose of everyone on the expedition, including me, is to support him and his work, yet not even his basic needs are being met. Now thick, acrid smoke from the wet wood begins to burn his eyes. This is the last straw.

Max complains bitterly and I turn my full attention toward his situation. As soon as the tents are up he changes clothes, but what can I do about the smoke? The Bahinemos built this shelter the same way as all the other shelters they have built; with a simple upside down "V" roof. I try to explain to them that if the plastic on one side of the roof is lifted higher and made to overlap that of the other side, it would let out the smoke but not let in the rain. They are too tired and hungry to follow my directions and don't understand. They have no tradition of building plastic houses, and they also find the smoke extremely uncomfortable. Traditionally smoke from their fires has always filtered out through palm fronds.

Everyone's eyes hurt. We all just want to eat, put the fires out and get to bed. Max begins to yell. Soon he is hollering and screaming at everyone, blaming the carriers for getting us into the whole situation. He is particularly angry that there is still nothing being done about the smoke. He keeps commanding me to tell the carriers to get rid of it. But we need the smoky fire to warm and dry ourselves and to fix a meal.

"I've had all I can take," he says. "I'm going to get out of here as soon as its day!"

"But San Edie, we can't build a whole new shelter in the dark. We have no materials. And how can we open up the roof without the rain pouring down through the hole? Doesn't he realize everyone's eyes are hurting and that we would fix it, if we could, even for ourselves? Can't he put up with an irritation?"

"An irritation!" Max bellows when I translate all of this. "This isn't an irritation; this is an emergency. Don't they know the difference between a life-threatening situation and a minor irritation? Are they stupid or do they just not care?"

I beg both parties to stop. This argument is not fixing a thing and I am being torn between the two sides. We take the tarp the carriers are planning to use on the ground to protect their beds from bugs and hang it as a curtain between the tents and the fire. It helps a little and we set out our bowls on the bare ground by a battery lamp so we can see to eat.

I had set aside a special meal of instant mashed potatoes and canned ham for this day, having suspected it might be difficult. Only the freeze dried green beans need to be boiled. We use the water from the beans to pour over the potato flakes. Some packets of potatoes are labeled "onion flakes". I select one with this added luxury for Max.

Our lamp attracts tiny gnats and these begin to fall into the plates full of food. They look just like the onion flakes. Somebody mentions the gnats just as Max receives his plate full of potato flakes scattered with more little brown dots than anyone else's. I don't know if any bugs really do fall in his potatoes or not, but he goes to bed without food.

Max's share of the food isn't wasted, however.

Crossing the river by log

A flower in a bright place

Chapter 20

The Eye Leech

~~ The screams of my little sister rang out through the palm stem walls. I couldn't bear to watch. Mom tried pouring cold water in her eyes but she only screamed louder. "There is something crawling in my eye," she yelled. But Mom didn't believe her until she saw it.~~

The exhausted Bahinemos go to bed at 10:00 pm right after the rest of us. They put the fire out early so they can pull the tarp down in order to set up their own tents and sleeping mats. Karl tries to hang his jungle hammock, but in the rain and dark he hangs it upside down. He keeps twisting it the right way but each time he gets in it, as soon as he dozes off, the hammock flips back around and he finds himself rudely awakened on the mud below. Four times of this, and he comes cussing and swearing into the shelter. He sets his hammock up like a tent on the tarp with the carriers.

Rob keeps putting his hips or his legs down through our platform made of rotten bark. I wake up every three hours trying not to scream from the itching rash while I wait for the next dose of Benadryl to take effect. It is a long night.

In the morning, comfort becomes our primary obsession. More important than improving the camp, however, is making sure some carriers will bring the rest of our supplies down from Gipa. Gogomo, Wamseli, Mathew and Jim come to me with a suggestion.

"We would like to send San Bahio and San Yamu to Wagu village today. They could gather some extra young men from the village to help carry tomorrow. Meanwhile, we have considered all of the items we left behind. We are convinced that four of us men can bring those supplies back by ourselves. What do you think?" they ask.

I agree that getting more workers from Wagu would help. They could bring in their own food for the night and help us all get out the next day. We only have a little food left and a lot of supplies that need to be carried out to Wagu.

I prefer that only one woman go to Wagu, however. Perhaps she could be accompanied by Ma Lekim who is still in some pain and unable to be of much help. I think we need as many people as possible to stay and improve the camp. But the Bahinemos don't seem to want their wives to navigate a trail alone, even with Lekim, perhaps in case he collapses. I am not sure, however, that they are right about the four carriers who are to travel back upriver being able to handle all of the stuff left at Gipa. They are so eager to enact their plan. I decide maybe their enthusiasm might make up for them being short-handed and I accept the plan.

The two parties depart immediately. The four men go back up river to Gipa and the two women head for Wagu. This leaves the camp to the monotonous drone of the cicadas and the steamy, morning sun. San Moyali, Ma Lekim and the child, Clement, are the only Bahinemos left in camp. Karl, Max and Rob are here with me also. Moyali and I wash the dishes. Then we gather some fruits to feed to the two baby cassowaries. They have cried "fweeeep, fweeeep" from the minute dawn broke. Unfortunately, the fruit doesn't do much to deter the "fweep"ing.

When Max crawls out of bed late, Moyali and I gasp. His eyes are swollen to the size of walnuts. He wasn't kidding when the night before he labeled the smoke a "serious" situation. He can't take photos like this.

Karl goes down to the only patch of sandbar on the river and begins weaving a cage out of rattan for his big baby chick. The sandbar widens steadily with each hour of the sun.

Ma Lekim takes Clement into the forest to teach him how to chop down and debark a large palm tree. The tree provides enough fresh bark to improve our bed and even make a raised bed for Ma Lekim himself. Seeing the bark peeled away from the trunk, however, is almost like watching someone skin an animal. He killed the tree to give us its coat.

I believe our time on the mountain built a significant bond between me and all the carriers. Moyali and I spend the rest of the morning washing muddy clothes for the whole camp. This gives me a chance to find out where she, as the primary landowner, stands on the issue of logging. Now that my language and culture skills have improved and she has learned to trust me, I am able at long last to have a real heart to heart talk with this person who is so important for saving the forest.

"Some of us have remained determined not to sell our trees to loggers ever since we learned it would destroy our forest," Moyali says. "Others believe the government representative with his promises of new preservation methods.

"Actually, the people of the Bahinemo village of Yigai are the only ones whom I know for certain will be giving up their land for logging. One of their men died in the hospital in Wewak. They had no way to pay for the return of his body. The government representative was kind enough to take care of it. Now, of course, they are obligated to repay him, and the only thing he wants is permission to log." Yigai is a much smaller Bahinemo village than Wagu. There is two other villages, Gahom and Inalu on the other side of Mount Hunstein. I have no idea what they think about logging.

"What about your land; this land we are on?" I want to know, realizing at the same time that such an event could easily sway her plans.

"My mind is firm," Moyali replies. "All of the land west of here is to be set aside as a wildlife refuge. It will connect with land that another clan has set aside for the same purpose. The area to the south, which we have walked over on this trip, is to be used for expeditions, both research and tourism," she assures me.

I would like to be truly reassured, but her plan is so tailored to my desires. My parents did much to help her village for many years. Does she think she owes us a debt? Could a logging company create an even greater debt? When the time comes, will she be able to resist conforming to the desires of other, less noble ventures? I am not sure. The situation is so fragile that it causes pain in my heart too deep for me to deal with. There is nothing I can do about it, anyway.

We are interrupted by a frantic yell from Karl. A week earlier he had complained about a little dirt in his eye. I gave him some filtered water to rinse his eye out and heard nothing more about it. I didn't know it had continued to itch. He and Ma Lekim were sitting on the beach trying to figure out why Karl's cage plan wasn't working, when suddenly Lekim spotted a half inch leech crawling around in Karl's eye. Karl looks as if he is going to be sick.

Rob runs to the first aid kit for tweezers. With them, I chase the parasite around. Soon sweat is pouring down Karl's face. Although I keep insisting he look the other way, the goal is impossible as each time I grab the leech, it squeezes out from between the pointy tweezers and scurries to the other side of the eye. Soon my tiny work place fills with tears. I don't blame Karl a bit. At last I catch the little beast and give it to Karl, who promptly divides it into almost microscopic pieces with his machete.

After lunch both Karl and Max feel their eyes are sufficiently recovered to take some photographs of the forest near the camp.

Ma Lekim asks Max if he needs us to build him a separate shelter. Max declines graciously. We can't restructure the roof of the main shelter, but Lekim and I prop up the tarpaulins on one side of the shelter's peak pulling them over and above the tarpaulins on the other side creating a covered gap in the peak of the roof, just in case it starts raining again. Meanwhile, since the weather is dry, Moyali keeps the fire out from under the tarpaulins and dries a stash of firewood. It seems unlikely that last evening's disaster will repeat itself.

Rob and I explore the river upstream from the sandbar and then float back down to a splendid, giant tree just below camp. Its massive three and a half foot diameter trunk leans way out over the water so I can almost walk up it and decide to try. When I reach the first branches I am about twenty feet above the river. I am feeling much better but the Benadryl I am on makes me a little too queasy for climbing, especially since the water is quite shallow underneath me. I back my way down. We switch to amateur photography. Rob tries to capture some of the myriad of butterflies which hover around our camp.

The four Bahinemo men who went back up river to Gipa had reassured us they would be back by mid-afternoon. We keep looking and listening. But they do not return.

Late in the afternoon Bahio and Yamu, the two women who went to Wagu for more workers, return with a man named Waga and his son. Some teenagers have come too, they tell us, but they will spend the night downriver at a garden camp with permanent huts called Galifa.

Bahio is exhausted, but at the same time proud and excited. She caught an even smaller baby cassowary on her way to Wagu. She left it with friends in the village, but she tells and retells the story with gusto. She brought a huge load of squashes, pineapples and beetle nut. Beetle nut is a seed which, when chewed, emits a mild, addictive drug. When I see all this, I understand the men's eagerness to send the women for reinforcements.

We make supper, but the guys are still not back. This time they took emergency flashlights with them. But what could be keeping them? Even with flashlights, hiking in a rainforest at night can be harrowing.

Rob and Max go on to bed and the women move the campfire back under the edge of the shelter for security and warmth. This does cause some smoke to waft through the shelter again, but the hole in the roof helps, and no one complains, so I don't try to stop them.

Well after dark, we finally hear a distant yodel from the far side of the river. Four guys stagger in with only one pack.

They wolf down their food from home and all the Papua New Guineans congregate around the campfire. Jim leans against his wife Bahio, a rare sight in Bahinemo culture, but he is exhausted and in pain. He has pulled his shoulders badly. The four men, Jim, Wamseli, Gogomo and Mathew, are so stiff they can hardly move. As the pile of beetle nut is reduced to a mound of red spit, the stories come forth:

"We got up to Gipa just as it began to rain and immediately realized we had made a mistake," Jim admits. "The load was far bigger than what any of us had remembered."

"There were two steel suitcases full of heavy cameras which we needed to carry on a pole between two men because of their weight and awkwardness. Plus, there were two loaded backpacks and two large luggage bags. In addition, there was a box we had completely forgotten about," he says.

They all take turns or join together to tell the rest of the story.

"First, we stuffed all of the goods from the box into the two backpacks, stretching their seams. We thought two of us could carry those. Then we tried to put the two luggage bags on the pole with the heavy camera trunks. The two men carrying the pole made it about twenty minutes down the trail to the first river crossing. Then the pole broke.

"Next, Gogomo tried to carry a luggage bag and a metal suitcase by himself, and Jim took on a backpack and the other luggage bag. This left just a backpack and camera trunk for Wamseli and Mathew; but that backpack stuffed with extra goods from the box, broke its straps.

"So Gogomo carried both steel camera cases by himself, and Jim carried both luggage bags by himself, while the other two tried to fix the backpack that broke. Gogomo went several feet this way and collapsed. Jim damaged his back, and the backpack continued to break loose."

After this the men decided to build a raft. None of them had an axe. To make the raft, they hacked several large trees into chunks with mere machetes. It rained steadily. Hours later, they were ready to tie the trees together with vines. They dragged the cargo one item at a time to the river's edge and loaded it onto the raft. As soon as the last item was carefully set afloat, the entire raft keeled over and neatly dropped its load into the river. The men dived in and managed to retrieve it all.

It began to rain harder. The river level got higher and higher and it was nearly dark. To save the luggage and themselves, the men decided to build a sapling platform with a palm leaf roof to store the luggage over-night. They rushed around the forest in the rain and dusk to gather materials. When it was finally finished, they secured the luggage to the platform with vines in case of flood. Then they selected a few items which they thought might be urgent and trudged through the darkness to the safety of our camp. They would have to return the next day with more men.

Chapter 21

Impossible Trail

~~ His hand was gangrenous, but
nothing would arouse the aid-post orderly to
take care of it, so at seventeen I soaked his
hand in salt-water and bandaged it with
antibiotics as best I could.~~

After hearing the men's story, I crawl into bed, but it is difficult to sleep. Once again, smoke accumulates in the shelter, but the men are too tired to hang up the ground cloth and too keyed up to doze off. On top of that, the betel nut is making them high. Their talking gets louder and louder, their stories more animated. The two baby cassowaries, confused by the light, won't stop crying loudly and harshly, "Fweeeep.... Fweeeeep.... Fweeeep." Finally at midnight I demand some courtesy to those in bed.

In the morning the sun never comes out. In fact it pours and pours. The sandbar disappears ten feet under the current, and everything in camp is dismal and soaked. The women stoke up the fire to get warm, and I boil our last oatmeal. Smoke billows inward.

Max loses his temper all over again. In addition to the smoke, he hadn't slept until midnight, either. "Why didn't someone make me a separate house yesterday?" he demands.

"But we asked and you said you were fine," we remind him.

He is inconsolable. He loudly laments that we are finished with our work in the rainforest and should be on the trail to Wagu at once. He can't take another minute here under any conditions, let alone the present ones.

I am concerned about Max, but I also feel responsible for seeing to the recovery of our abandoned supplies. When Max hears the story about the supplies at Gipa, he isn't the slightest bit amused. He does say his camera trunks are *supposed* to be waterproof, but does that guarantee allow for torrential down-pours and being dunked in rivers? I tell Max that I want to wait in Bani to be sure his equipment is still OK, but that doesn't phase him. He wants out of the whole mess. At that point Rob and I understand he really has had all he can take, but is leaving for Wagu even possible in this rain?

Bahio discovered the day before that more fallen trees than anyone can remember have blocked the old route to Wagu. We will have to go down-river to Galifa and then cross the ridge between there and Wagu. It will take longer, and because of the rain, this new river trail will be fraught with flooded creeks and slippery logs. Beyond them, the ridge will be dangerously steep while covered in mud. Dangerous or otherwise, we have to get out sooner or later.

Just then, the group of boys who spent the night camped at Galifa arrives. I see immediately that there are enough of them to get our equipment back before noon. I demand that all those who can swim cross the river right away toward our abandoned gear. Maybe the weather will clear after lunch and allow us all to leave for Wagu when they get back.

The rain continues.

Around 11:00 AM, Ma Lekim informs me we will not be leaving Bani at all that day. "You can't hike in the rainforest in this kind of weather, San Edie, it's extremely dangerous!"

"Dangerous? What is dangerous about it?" demands Max when I interpret this news. "Why, this is only an irritation. They just don't want to walk in the rain."

At this the carriers begin to yell, "What is the matter with this man? Doesn't he know the difference between a life threatening situation and a minor 'irritation'? Is he stupid or does he just not care?"

If only they could understand each other's languages! They are saying the exact same things about Max regarding walking in the rain that he said about them regarding the smoke. I can't believe it. I am getting tired of taking the brunt of both sides since all of their yelling is directed at me, the interpreter. For a few minutes I walk away.

When I calm down, I discuss the problem with Rob and we both agree we have to get Max out. He has reached his reasonable limit and is on the verge of a complete breakdown. I go to Ma

Lekim again and tell him Max and I will be leaving that day if there is any way out at all.

"We won't let you," Ma Lekim informs me solemnly. "None of our people are willing to accompany you. If you want to go by yourselves, go ahead. You will spend the night in mud in the forest." Ma Lekim is not angry at me. He is very concerned.

I sit and think. While I do, Max paces back and forth muttering to everyone including himself. Realizing he is a complete captive in the place has put him right at the edge of his sanity. But I don't know which is worse; to keep him in the bugs, rain and smoke another night, or watch him collapse on a dangerous trail trying to leave.

Wamseli is mature enough to have good judgment regarding the condition of the trail, but young enough not to feel responsible for his every word as Ma Lekim does, with his authority as an elder. I think he might be more frank with me about the pros and cons of traveling that day.

"Solomon (Lekim) is right, San Edie," he says. "That trail is nearly impossible in the rain." I explain our situation. "If this was an ordinary rain, you could go," he replies. "Anybody can walk in the rain. But if it rains all night and all day as it has, then the whole trail can become a wreck. Unless the weather clears up completely, you haven't a chance to make it to Wagu."

That is a glimmer of hope for me. What if it does clear?

"By what time would it have to clear up completely in order for us to go back today?" I ask.

Wamseli looks at me with a mixture of alarm and amusement, but practically thinks through the timing before giving his answer. "I believe if the sun comes out before 1:00 PM, and you leave at exactly 1:30, you *might* be able to arrive at the lake by dark. That is *if* Max walks as fast as he can and never stops to rest." I look at Wamseli, and I look at Max. Then I sit on the edge of our bark bed to wait and pray for the weather.

At 1:00 pm, the sun bursts through the clouds. We can't believe it and run out of the shelter to check the whole sky. Indeed, most of it is blue. In no time everything is packed. Six teenage boys are willing to accompany Rob, Max and me. Karl stays to take care of our cargo which has not yet returned from the makeshift shelter on the way from Gipa.

I give Moyali my last bag of rice and she assures me everyone will move to the garden as soon as the men come down river. There will be plenty of squashes to eat there. She cries, puts her hand on my shoulder and gives me her special walking stick as a token of good will and faith that we will all safely reunite. "Return it to me tomorrow," she says.

I strap my fanny pack around my waist, with lunch and some basic first aid, and sling a bottle of water over my shoulder. Then I go to Ma Lekim and kneel down next to him. "I am sorry that I must go against you this time," I say. "I have been commissioned to take care of Max and I must go with him. I don't want you to think I have been disrespectful or disregarded your advice. I realize we will be walking in danger."

Ma Lekim smiles a tender, concerned, but satisfied smile. "Go with my blessing, San Lekim," he says, using his related name for me again. "You are doing your job well."

With shoes tied to my belt in readiness for the steep ridge, I press my bare feet into the mud and cross the creek. The others are already far ahead, but it's easy to find their trail on the mud flats.

The forest is dark, and for some it would have been gloomy, especially alone, but I find in it solemn, mysterious beauty. The canopy is so thick that the sky can't be seen, but rather appears mottled green. Strange shapes where currents have come and gone lie in the mud packed around logs and in gullies. In some places the mud takes on an orange glow which matches nicely with the green sky and brown trunks.

I catch up to Rob, Max and the six boys. Walking in a stretched out line, we cross many creeks and mud gullies, and head deeper and deeper into the forest. After nearly an hour we come back to the edge of the river and find it brown and swollen from bank to bank. Large drops of rain begin to fall.

From the river we angle toward the side of a ridge, crossing many creeks which are now filled to waist level. Most are bridged by dead limbs, but these are not strong enough to hold the weight of a European man. Nor are they wide enough for one to balance on, so

Max and Rob often have to wade. The teenaged boys who are our guides lend an encouraging hand now and then, but they walk in absolute, eerie silence.

Soon we are required to cross several small rivers, each time balancing tediously over narrow, slippery logs while the current swirls below. I look at Max, but it seems nothing can daunt him. He is determined to prove our condition a mere "irritation" and to get out of the rainforest. I am grateful for this motivation. There is no time for complications.

The rivers continue to rise until water covers our ankles, even on the trail. A large cassowary thuds away from us in the dark distance. Another time we startle a Victoria Crown Pigeon. It flutters up into the canopy with its wings making a loud "click, click, click" sound.

At last we cross a narrow strip of foul swamp and enter the downriver garden camp, Galifa. It is a regular Western ghost town. There are five or six complete houses, though rather than having walls, their palm leaf roofs go clear to the floor on two sides like A-frames. Their floors are made of sturdy bark and are on stilts, about six feet off the ground above the bugs. There is a large fire-place in the center of the circle of houses. The night before, the teenage boys left the charred remains of a squash feast scattered around each house.

All around the houses the large "garden" is recognizable only by its absolute denseness in comparison with the open rainforest. Taro plants loom eight feet high, and squash vines climb trees. Tobacco plants and banana trees are mixed in like weeds. Every inch is billowing greenery. The only way to navigate it is to walk carefully, balancing along the lengths of the whitened logs of the original forest, which now lie like ghostly grid work above the ground.

We have passed out of flood level and the rain stops, so we rest a few minutes and eat some cookies I have saved. Our guides say very little and I wonder what they are thinking.

From the houses, the guides lead us to wade in a stony creek. This takes us directly to the steep ridge between us and Wagu. We ascend right away.

The forest is dark and still. The path is steep indeed, but well-worn. A baby snake slithers under my feet as I climb the side of a sloping gully.

Rob and Max make jokes about the trip being "Edie's guaranteed weight-loss program." A closer look at Max makes me realize he has indeed lost weight in two weeks.

The wide path zigzags back and forth up the ridge. It is well established and easy to follow. We cheer up when we look behind us at a beautiful view of the next ridge over. When we cross the top of our own ridge I press ahead, hoping to spend a few minutes alone enjoying a good view of the lake. The trail leads me down the trunk of a steep log which I find as slippery as ice. I fall twice, both times recovering myself by sliding into shrubbery. Here on the down hill slope is the serious danger. This is what Ma Lekim was so concerned about.

Dusk is approaching with its tropical swiftness. I worry about the time. A dreadful sago swamp lies ahead between the bottom of the ridge and the lake. If we make it past the swamp and reach the lake, there will still be a long way to go. Canoeing across the lake in the dark to Wagu could take hours. That is assuming the women and boys left paddles and dugout canoes for us to use to get across the lake. Before I think of any alternatives if there are no boats, the others catch up to me.

I can tell by their concerned faces and muddy clothes that they have also fallen once or twice. We continue on in hurried silence.

Suddenly, I hear Rob yell and turn around to see him with his leg jammed under a log. He pulls it out, but it's covered with blood. A six inch gash runs down the front of his right shin. I fumble in his pack for the gauze. There is little left, but somehow I must protect the wound from the filth ahead. I do my best and wrap it thin.

We cover a few more yards. Then we hear a horrid, muffled cry from a shy, young man up ahead. Rob and I look down the trail, confused to see him lying across it. We hurry to his side, arriving just as he begins to get his wits about him. Blood is spurting everywhere from his hand. He fell on his machete and sliced the space between his thumb and forefinger to the bone. I search for the last gauze and tape from Rob's pack. All I can do is bandage it tight.

When the bleeding stops, I try to carry the young man's load so we can go on. It's a steel drying rack loaded with Karl's plants and is both awkward and heavy. Rob takes it from me, handing me his smaller pack, and we resume our hurried descent toward the fetid, thorn filled, malarial swamp below.

Twilight arrives suddenly just as we reach the bottom of the ridge. We immediately enter the swamp. No one stops or hesitates. Strange eerie palms armored with six inch thorns surround us. Their giant fronds appear to grope together in the dusky half-light. Stinking foam-coated mud lies spread around us waist deep. We press on. No one wants to wait for anyone else in a race against malaria loaded mosquitoes. Yet keeping up with the person in front is essential, as the trail disappears quickly in the sticky ooze.

With each step, I feel carefully around for branches hidden under the surface of the mud, which create the trail. If I miss them, I can barely lift my legs above the mire. Rob and Max, I notice, keep falling in up to their thighs. Are they so much heavier? They don't complain, but push on through the deepening shadows.

At last, we reach the edge of the lake. There, to our tremendous relief, is the glorious sight of a twenty foot motorized canoe. Jacob, the boatman whom Rob hired to take him to Wagu, has anticipated our return date and has been waiting at the mouth of the trail for the last two days. We are safe at last.

At night as we lie secure and dry under our musty mosquito net, my husband asks me how I managed to keep from sinking into the swamp up to my thighs like Max and him.

"I guess the sticks were just barely strong enough to hold me up with a little pack, but not you with a heavy one," I reply.

"Sticks? What sticks?" he exclaims. That's when I realize neither he nor Max knew to search for the submerged semi-floating stick trail which was trampled down about six inches into the mud. They had both floundered through the ooze unaided, while I sank in only to my ankles.

View from high above forested hills

The muddled jungle of a garden

Chapter 22

A Different Point of View

~~ Being raised in Papua New Guinea
and living in the U.S.A. as an adult created a
great deal of cultural confusion within me.~~

In my parents' old house we sleep right through the howling dogs, the neighbors' chatter, the frogs, the bats and even the obnoxious rooster. In the morning after oatmeal, coffee and slices of red papaya, we can't wait to take the canoe to Ambunti, the small town with the air-strip. Rob's wide gash turns out to be only skin deep, but the boy with the cut hand needs to get to a hospital. We also need supplies. The bread, butter and fresh, red meat which I ordered months in advance sound gourmet. Our missionary friends promised to hold them for us in their freezer.

Before we leave, however, Max and I have one last disagreement. "I am so glad you brought me out yesterday," he begins, "and pleased that I was right about the wet trail being no more than an inconvenience. As you can see, there was no danger after all."

"I doubt very much if that opinion is shared by the boy with the cut hand," I respond, offended by this final act of apparent insolence. "Bahinemo men don't fall on trails, and I know such a wound would never have happened had it not been for our ill-regarded trip."

"So you're going to blame me for that accident," Max replies, shocked at the connection. "I think it's time for me to leave." His voice carries an air of resolution and indignance. "What other photos are absolutely necessary?" he asks.

There is nothing more to say about the matter. Obviously, we are viewing things through opposing cultural prisms. At least he will try to finish the magazine's goals.

I suggest that a series on the women gathering sago from the palms in the swamp we have just survived could be done in one day. That, plus a boat trip up the lower Hunstein River to see flood plain forest would cover the essentials. After that, Max can leave. I am amazed and impressed that he immediately arranges a guide to take him back into the fetid sago swamp that very day, while Rob and I go to town.

The trip down the river toward Ambunti is beautiful. It washes over the dark, confusing trials of the last few days in the forest like waves on a sandy beach. Fluffy white clouds and a cool morning breeze soften the sun. The green marsh we travel through extends all the way to a distant low horizon of blue hills. The water of the channel is smooth and deep, and mirrors the scenery perfectly. Several beautiful white-bellied sea eagles glide along just ahead of us, hunting whatever our boat scares up. Flocks of herons, egrets and cormorants watch us from tall trees. Occasionally other exotic birds, such as a bright red and green eclectus parrot or a pair of tiny pygmy geese, put in their appearance. We pull up at the Ambunti dock, as ready to taste civilization again as children craving popsicles on a hot day.

Our missionary friends, Doug and Leah Heideman of Pacific Island Ministries, open their home and treat us like relatives. As we arrive, Leah sets plates of real sandwiches in front of us and tall glasses of lemonade, then eggs and bacon, then fruit salad, and so on. I realize how much I have missed the company of fellow Westerners when I notice I am talking, talking and talking.

The first thing we do after our delicious lunch is borrow the Heideman's truck and take our friend to the hospital. However, when we get there we are told the whole hospital is closed until some thieves return the hospital outboard motor. No amount of pleading produces a doctor. Deciding it's too late for stitches anyway, we return to the mission to tend the wound ourselves. I can only imagine the mess it will be.

Papua New Guinea is the most Christian nation in the entire world, with 94% of the population professing to be born-again Christians. To them the Gospel is a solution to a host of terrors, not a list of rules. They have good morals in their own cultures, but they live in fear of evil spirits and vengeful, ancestral ghosts until missionaries tell them God can protect them from those things. Of course, many less noble aspects of Western "Christian" culture are adopted as well. It is hard for anyone to sort it all out.

The night before, an eccentric PNG pastor who had come with our driver from another village had dinner with us at Wagu. He preached long and loud at us throughout our whole meal. This culminated in a dramatic, even if slightly irritating, prayer over our young carrier's deep cut.

I slowly and gingerly unwrap the gauze. To our utter amazement, a thin sealed line on the skin is all that indicates there was a cut. There will hardly be a scar. Was this the result of the odd pastor's prayer, I wonder?

In the afternoon a ruffled tourist, a professor of primitive art, knocks on the mission door. He is made as welcome as we are. "I just arrived in town yesterday afternoon," he informs us, "from the most awful, backwards, indignant, rude place I have ever set foot in, in all of my world travels."

"And where might that be?" we naturally wonder, and don't hesitate to ask.

"It's a little village called 'Wagu' on the edge of Wagu lake," he exclaims, completely unaware of our association.

"So what was it that was so terrible?" we ask.

"Well," he replies with dismay, "the people did not treat me as a guest, but completely expected me to fend for myself. When I asked them if I could buy a baby cassowary, they quoted me the outrageous price of $5,000. They seemed to have no idea how to relate to tourists at all."

We introduce ourselves and I explain that the Wagu people do not think of any race as better than any other, and they have no intention of selling their cassowaries. "How would you like it if a stranger approached you and questioned the price of your car, or your daughter's favorite horse?" I ask him. After more mutual enlightenment, we part amicably.

In anticipation of tomorrow's trip up the lower Hunstein River, we arrange to hire a sturdy aluminum flat-bottom "river truck" instead of the canoe. As the boat noses its way back toward Wagu late in the afternoon with fresh supplies, I think about Max and the tourist.

Poor Max endured blood-sucking leeches, fiery bees and camps without schedules or tables. He ate soup with seeds that needed to be spit out after each bite, and spent days fording rivers and traipsing through knee high mud. He spent hours focusing a camera to turn flowers into art while bugs he had previously never dreamed of focused on the back of his neck. He slept in raging torrents. He endured days of joining only those conversations which he specifically asked to have translated. All in all his patience is truly amazing. My Western side is returning.

It is almost impossible to comprehend that the rainforest part of our trip is over. While I enjoyed the contact with Americans and the wonderful refreshments, there is also a deep sadness in me. I miss the rainforest already. Real rainforest is so self-contained that you are either in it, or you aren't. It never gives you a chance to say good-bye. You can't get rid of part of it, like a few species, or some trees, or it completely unravels. One minute it's there in all its glory. The next minute it's completely absent, like a friend who has died. You can't play with it like men do the beach, or build towns in it like the desert. Wagu was a rainforest when I was a child. Now it's a village.

I am brought back to the present when I notice that the boat stops gliding sideways around hairpin loops and is following a straight channel. Moments later we skim around the end of a last ridge and the blue hills of the Hunstein Range open up before us. We are out of the marsh and sailing across Wagu Lake.

I wonder if Karl and the rest of our team are out of those hills yet. I wonder if the rain ever stopped in Bani, and whether Ma Lekim made it out. I wonder about Max's baptized equipment.

When we pull up to the Wagu shore, Karl, Moyali, Gogomo, Bahio and all the rest are waiting for us. Bahio is crying, but this turns out to be because she has just learned her baby cassowary died. They all brim with stories about a harrowing night of complex jungle maneuvers and a shortage of food.

I rush up the path to the house to see how Max survived the swamps and being alone in the village. I find him cleaning cameras from the two metal cases that sank in the river in Gipa. He is quite pleased. Sealed inside, they are unscathed.

In fact, Max had a very successful day. He hiked around in the muddy sago swamp taking photos all morning long, then walked back to the village to make himself a soup lunch. After this he returned to the swamp in a new location and took many more photos of the sago process. He hired a woman to wash out his clothes, and is jolly to learn Rob has brought the part which is needed to fix the bucket shower. He is his old, happy self again.

We learn that Ma Lekim and some of the women and children at Bani walked to the Galifa "garden" soon after we did on the same rainy day. The men gathered our straggling supplies from both Gipa and Bani together on a raft and floated them to Galifa that afternoon. This new raft was so large that the rest of the carriers clambered aboard with our supplies. Their worst misadventure was a giant python, which at one point hung precariously over the river from a fallen tree. Reportedly, all had abandoned ship, leaving the raft to lodge itself under the log, company to the python. Gogomo saved the day by swimming underwater and pushing the raft through the jam all by himself.

On their way to Galifa, the campers had looked forward to a dinner of roast squashes. However, when they arrived at Galifa, they discovered that the teenage boys had completely devoured all of the squashes the night before. They found no additional food in our supplies on the raft. The two pound bag of rice I had given Moyali was the only food that sustained the entire party of eighteen.

Maybe it was good that we had left on Max's schedule, after all. I don't know if I could have handled twenty-four hours more on only a tablespoon of rice.

Chapter 23

Cultural Collision

~~ *"Wa-oh-wa-oh-wa-ee-ya." The music floated in waves across the night air, and wrapped around the steady thump of drums. Drops of sweat ran under the paint that covered my face and arms as I stood at the edge of the circle and stared at the orange glow flickering across the surreal faces bouncing and swaying in circles before me. Men had bones and shells through their noses. The multi-colored designs on their faces under the elaborate bouquets of feathers in their hair, and the altering shadows, made individuals almost unrecognizable. At five years old I felt apprehensive as I waited in the shadows outside the ring of chanters. However, I wouldn't think of missing what everyone had been carefully preparing for and waiting for all month.*

Before I knew what was happening, I was swept up and thrown onto someone's back. I swayed back and forth as she rocked me around and around the circle, holding my leaf clad chest tightly against her back to avoid losing me in the fray. Leaves and feathers bounced everywhere around me. Red paint dripped down my face. Shells clacked and jingled on hips, shoulders and necks. The

melody of the chant rose and fell and pulsed
loudly into the dark, but the rhythm and
melody were natural and comforting. ""Wa-
oh-wa-oh-wa-ee-ya." ~~

We are invited to join the village in a "sing-sing", or all night dance. When night falls men place a lantern on a pole at the top of the village and people begin to sing and dance around it in a swaying manner. Men jump with enthusiasm around the outside circle, leading the songs in forceful full voices. Skirts swing gaily around the center of the ring. The women's voices echo the men's in lilting harmony.

One or two people dress all out. They cover themselves with beads, clay, colorful feathers, and leaves. Most, however, only tuck a few leaves into their clothes or a feather into their hair. Many are not dressed up at all. Where did the beauty and intensity I remember from my youth go?

To my surprise it soon becomes apparent there are two sing-sings: the Bahinemo sing-sing in the village square, and a wedding dance in the style of the neighboring Kagiru people. It is literally in full swing in a relative's house. Although the village is now well represented by Kagirus, when I travelled to their village at age 17, I and the other girls in our party were the first white females the Kagirus had ever seen and they stroked our long hair and patted our skin with awe. We traded cartridges with them for arrows stained with the blood of animals.

People wander back and forth between the two dances depending on the choice of songs and where the most fun seems to be taking place. I decide to look in on the new Kagiru sing-sing. The wood and vine frame of the house rocks and bounces in time to the music. The air is hot and stuffy as wall to wall bodies either watch or join the singing and dancing. This sing-sing is only for women, and instead of walking around in a circle, they leap from one foot to the other. Colorful grass skirts sway pendulum style. Arms wave in the air. As the women dance, sweat pours off their faces and bare chests. They close their eyes tight and sing with strong animated voices. Here is the fervor I remember in Bahinemo dances from my childhood. I am perplexed at the enthusiasm in this Kagiru sing-sing versus the apathy in the Bahinemo sing-sing.

Why have the villagers changed sing-sing styles? Why is their culture changing? The answer is, it has always been changing. Even before the advent of the white men the Bahinemo culture was becoming extinct on its own. Their old way of life, which included sorcery instead of medicine; revenge instead of politics; and on-going war, was so harsh and so precarious and terrifying that they died much faster than they could reproduce. Illness and war claimed lives all the time, so some things about their culture needed to change.

I dance at the Kagiru sing-sing until 1:00 am. As is true for about half of the other women there, I don't speak the language, and so do not know the songs, but the choruses are repeated often and are easy to pick up. From time to time a few women sing out the verses and we all come in on the chorus, creating an echo effect. One of my friends tells me the songs alternate between slow, sad songs of a mother mourning the loss of her daughter, and light, fast, cheerful songs about the bride's ensuing life with her husband. The women act out some of the cheerful songs. Some songs contain hysterical words with double meanings and sarcasm, making fun of men's ways.

Both sing-sings continue throughout the night. The Kagiru wedding goes on until 3:00 pm the next afternoon.

However, women stay with the Kagiru bride and do not allow her to consummate the marriage until the bride and groom undergo a brief Western ceremony the next day. This is the bride and groom's incongruous choice.

There have to be changes. Whether initiated by caring missionaries, like my folks, by awkward governments, selfish, manipulative traders, developers and fortune seekers, or even by gawking tourists, the outside world is due to arrive in full. Like the waves stirred up by a storm, change is rolling in, relentlessly pounding the village that stands in its way. One way or another, "progress" will throw the Bahinemos into a new world where many old ways mean nothing while education, politics, medicine and negotiating capitalism mean basic survival. Tradition no longer dictates. From now on the Bahinemos must make choices.

Chapter 24

The Question of Tourism

~~ "I don't think tourists would come here," Dr. Sohmer said. They would need air conditioners, power outlets, good screen protection and they wouldn't want to walk through the sago swamp to get to the river."~~

Saturday morning is bright and beautiful. Karl, Max and I, plus Jacob, the driver, pack up the boat with cameras, emergency supplies, plenty of film and a picnic.

Rob decides not to go with us up the Hunstein River from its mouth. He wants time to fix some of the Bahinemos' equipment. They have no mechanics and few tools so often technical items such as radios or lamps lie idle for months, lacking some simple, five minute procedure.

Jacob starts up the engine and we speed across the lake back toward the marshy channel that leads to town. After about twenty minutes, the river churns out of a gap in the marsh on the left. We turn onto it and feel the coolness of mountain water under our feet through the aluminum boat. As we careen back and forth around the bends of the narrow river, we are hidden in ten-foot high swamp grass.

Birds are so abundant that Max wants to stop and I have to remind him we need to go on into flood plain forest. A sea eagle follows our wake for a while. Brahminy kites, egrets, herons, bitterns, cormorants and ducks fill every tree we pass. Tiny weaver finches pack small bushes with nests.

Under the swamp grass, deep water spreads for miles in every direction. Scattered trees grow up out of the water on either side of the river, showing where land would be in the dry season. A wake in the channel as we round a bend indicates a crocodile has slipped off the grass and into the river. I remember my apprehension when, as a child, I was led in urgent whispers away from a large pile of wet hay on a sand bank in this river. Papua New Guinea crocodiles are elusive and almost never seen, but huge foot prints told us a guarding mother was near that nest.

There are more and more trees, until we are weaving through a tall maze of them, filled with brilliant screaming parrots and hung with gorgeous blossoming red lianas. Gradually the trees become a forest.

True floodplain forest is my favorite type of rainforest because of its abundant wildlife. Deep water covers it for months at a time deterring humans. In some places, hundreds of brightly colored lorries permeate the leaves like swarms of noisy bees. Both white cockatoos and rare black palm cockatoos fly in abundance over our heads thrilling us with their aerial acrobatics. Hornbills race away with loud whistling wings and honking cries as we round bends into their territories.

We have such a marvelous time. Like an audience at a fireworks display, we "Ooh" and "Aah" at every turn. After only one and a half hours, we come to a mass of freshly fallen trees. Their leaves are still green and clearly torn down by a storm. Our boat will not go around or over them. If we had brought an axe we could cut through them. The forest has shared with us all that it will share.

On our way back downriver we take our time photographing flowers, birds and butterflies. We get out of the boat and swim and float down the cool, tea colored water, resting only from log to log.

We are in an isolated tropical nature paradise only a couple of hours from the village.

<< >>

Andrew sits under his house on a carved wooden stool, rubbing his bare feet in the dust and gazing across the lake at deep blue sky and capering white clouds. He is the former village doctor. He comes from another tribe and is tall and dark. Several years earlier he tired of being a doctor and turned to politics. Now he is nursing a hangover from a habit picked up as the provincial government representative. Almost all government officials drink heavily. Andrew had a moderate PNG education and has been to Australia as a tourist.

"Where'd you go?" he asks me, referring to a quick jaunt in a dugout canoe which I took across a small bay to a nearby waterfall.

"We used to play there when I was a kid," I tell him.

"I've been thinking a lot about tourism," Andrew says. "You white people like things like that waterfall. I've got some ideas. We could build a lodge or something, either at the falls or over at Kakabu creek. We could set up nature walks, a little zoo. And the villagers could sell their carvings."

"The waterfall is closest to the village," I suggest, catching his vision. "That spot would be easier to service than the creek."

"Yes, I know. I thought about that, but the waterfall dries up for four months out of the year."

"That can't be," I reply. "When I was a child, when the whole lake dried up to a pool of mud, my Dad would take us over there in a canoe to bring back clean water to drink. The falls were full. We would swim in the creek right in the middle of the dry season." I can still feel the cool of stepping into the dark, lush green forest and hear the roar of the fresh water as it crashed down over the rock face. Then I remember the watershed principal.

"When people cut trees, the water ways will dry up," Dr. Sohmer had said.

"Why is the forest around the falls gone?" I ask Andrew suddenly.

"A fire came. We never had a fire before but it was a drought year. It never grew back like it was."

We compare notes further, and Andrew confirms that it has been since the fire that the falls have dried up. Learning of the waterfall's demise causes me deep pain. I dare not think about the whole forest being destroyed.

Andrew breaks into my reverie with more thoughts about tourism. The tribe adopted Andrew, like they did my family, for his guiding knowledge and because he chose to stay and get involved. He speaks English, although he prefers Tok Pisin. As the political representative of the village, it is Andrew's driving incentive to provide the village with some way to develop. Tourism is his main idea.

For years tourists have paid a large tour company $300 to $400 to come up the Sepik River with a small ship and send flatboats to visit Wagu village. None of this money reaches the Bahinemos. The tourists know nothing about the rainforest. They know nothing about Wagu. They come, stand and stare. They take a few pictures, then go back in their boats to the air conditioned ship. I once watched a line of tourists face a line of Bahinemos and simultaneously, each in their own language undecipherable to the other; discuss the absurdities of each other's clothing. "Can you imagine wearing a grass skirt with a gap in the sides?" "Can you imagine wearing a double knit pant-suit in this heat?" For this humiliation the villagers occasionally make a few dollars with the sale of a wooden carving.

Andrew and others in the country, like Harry Sakulas, believe there must be a way to attract tourists who will relate on a less colonial, more equal basis to the villagers and provide direct income for the Bahinemos themselves. Such income could replace logging. Perhaps the new focus of tourism needs to be the rainforest, rather than differences among people.

Westerners and tour companies as well as the villagers would need a lot of education to pull off eco-tourism. Would it even work? There would have to be many compromises. It seems out of the question.

I listen to Andrew describe his frustration at persuading the villagers to re-adopt their ancestral traditions so that tourists would come more often and take more pictures. For example they could go back to the old sing-sings or build a ceremonial tamboran house.

However, most of the traditions the tourists want, such as the building of a "haus tamboran," involve sorcery. When the villagers followed these traditions, they never did them because they were quaint, fun, cute, natural, or easy or even traditional. They did them because they were afraid of spirits, and they wanted to get spiritual power in their own hands rather than leave it in the hands of their enemies. They used the tamboran houses to discuss and carry out spiritual activities. For example, they might put a wall of ancestral spirits around the village in order to protect themselves from enemy spirits which cause sickness or death. The Bahinemos believe spirits inhabit the artistic carvings tourists love so much. The beautiful drum beats in their old sing-sings were a form of communicating with the spirit world.

The purpose of development is so they drop these old fears; get healthy by recognizing medicine, and get wealthy by working. There is a conflict here. In some ways tourism, mostly run by Australians, hasn't developed well in PNG because it has been defeating its purpose.

A simple illustration of the irony of tourism as development can be seen in the issue of the clothing worn at the sing-sing. "Why should we work for hours to make clothing out of raw materials for a sing-sing now that we have money and can buy cloth clothes?" the villagers ask. Virtually every person in the sing-sing had worn Western clothes under his or her decor. Tourists don't like that.

There are other frustrations. "I tell the village what we need to do to get tourism started and they all agree, but when it's time to act, no one shows up," Andrew tells me.

I decide to talk to Ma Lekim and Ma Gogomo about it. Ma Waga, who is Lekim's enterprising eldest son, is also there.

"Tourism is evil," Waga says. "As members of the church we can't support it."

"Why?" I ask, amazed. "What could make it wrong?"

"Evil spirit carvings decorate all tourist establishments and most are shaped like tamberan houses where men worship spirits. Besides that, they bring beer."

I had never thought about that, but they are right! In most countries, people go to hotels to vacation, attend conferences, and see new sights. Throughout PNG people primarily go to hotels to get drunk.

"We have enough problems with alcohol in the village as it is," they explain. "It has made our young men stop listening to us and is tearing up our families. The last thing we need is a steady stream of beer. But if we make a law that beer can't be sold at our lodge, tourists wouldn't come."

I wonder if tourism would bring in as much alcohol and prostitution as a big outside logging company. Are the forest and the villagers doomed to compromise?

Trees full of birds in the flooded forest

Dancing in a changing culture

Chapter 25

A Painful Goodbye

*~~Leaving for college in the U.S., I
didn't see how I could ever return to the
Hunstein. Tears streamed down my face as I
pulled away from the shore, and through
them, I saw that my young orange kitten, now
abandoned was swimming out after the boat*

.~~

The next day we pay the carriers without complications.
Then, we sell off our supplies as we won't need them in the U.S. I
can hardly face the last morning in Wagu. Bahio, Moyali, Jim,
Gogomo, Ma Lekim and others, have become an integral part of my
life. The days have gone by so fast. Visitors stop by in a constant
stream from early morning until deep into the night, but there are
still many friends I don't get to visit. We have no known way to plan
a return, though that is impossible for me to comprehend.

Max will take his pictures directly to *National Geographic*
and it is not likely that we will ever see him again once we are out of
the country.

All I can do for the Hunstein Rainforest is take a little piece
of it with me in the form of writing and photos to make my plea to
the world. Wagu and the rainforest are the Bahinemos'
responsibility. We will have to wait and see what happens. For the
moment, they are making good choices. We hope we have conveyed
the importance of saving the forest, if nothing else, by our closeness
to those who trekked with us. There will be many difficult choices
for them to make in the months ahead as development progresses.
One way or another, the Bahinemo culture must change. How will it
affect the rain forest? Both the rainforest and the culture, seem
equally delicate.

Several people volunteer to help clean the house and pack up
our things. We can't get through it without them.

The whole village lines up in a grand crowd along the shore where our boat is waiting. Friends grab my hands all the way into the boat. I can't speak. I don't want to think. Once again, a mere couple of hours will zap me right out of their world. My tears blur their faces as we pull away.

The boat cuts across the waters of the lake, leaving a long wake. We slowly trace the channel. I take in the ducks, the eagles, the reflected blue hills, the marsh grass and the sky, and try to pack them inside me, but they do not stay.

Too soon we turn onto the Sepik River and then pull ashore in Ambunti. Eventually, we make our way all the way to the capitol, Port Moresby, where we felt the earthquake ages ago. We call the kids and try to think of Dallas.

To ease our culture shock, Rob and I walk the tourist shops. The hotel store is filled with fascinating books as well as jewelry, intricate carvings, clothing and shells. We want everything.

In time, we argue too much over what to select and decide to try a swim in the pool. It is no use. We are both so tense that everything we do irritates the other. After a short time we go up to our room to talk things out. Suddenly, I look at him and he looks at me, and we both understand.

"You don't want to leave, do you, baby?" I say, fighting back tears.

"I never want to leave this country, Edie. You know that," he replies.

We hold each other for a while, gazing out of the balcony window at the flowers and the sunset and the sea. The long line of people along the shore wafts through my mind, their faces smiling through tears. White water billows up from a "thousand foot chasm," to the haunting echo of a bird-of-paradise. Then Gogomo sits on a high mountain waiting for me. A giant leaf floats down from the ceiling of an ancient green tree cathedral, and a flock of lorikeets scatters like fireworks above flooded trees.

Crying, we pack up our bags.

Early in the morning we walk a very long way across hot tarmac to an airplane labeled "Continental." On board, a sweet southern flight attendant gushes, "You mean y'all have lived in this country for a month and traveled around in it? Wow! What's it like?"

What's it like? What *is* it like…? My mind turns the question around over and over while I watch blue mountains covered with rich rainforest disappear into clouds thousands of feet below. I clutch an intricately carved wooden crocodile I just bought, feeling with my finger tips the scaly curves that speak of the life of an ancient creature disappearing stealthily into a misty rainforest. Like the crocodile the rainforest is slipping away: magnificent, wild and amazing.

Chapter 26

Dance of the Birds of Paradise

*~~"Sh sh sh!" the men said, finding it
difficult to keep us children from scaring the
birds away. They motioned for us to look
through a hole in the tall trees. There far
above us yellow and brown fur-like feathers
and green heads bobbed and twisted,
somersaulted and spun, cawed and whistled--
the dance of the Bird of Paradise.*

It's 2007. Fifteen years have passed since my rendezvous
with the Hunstein Rainforest. For fifteen years I have agonized over
whether the village is still intact or whether the rainforest and the
Bahinemo culture have slipped away. A family tragedy kept me
from being able to return to the rainforest or Wagu. I spoke to the
Bahinemos only once.

It was a year after I left. I was able to get a call through by
satellite phone to Ambunti and send a message on the next boat to
Wagu that I wanted the members of our expedition to call me. They
then had to charter a canoe to come in to Ambunti themselves,
where they borrowed a phone for several dollars. I immediately
called them back from the U.S. The reception was bad but Ma
Lekim's words to me came between sobs. "San Edie, please come
back and help us. Please… We need you!" I felt like I betrayed him;
betrayed all of them. Ma Lekim died shortly after that. I never
arranged a call again. It was too painful.

I tried writing letters but the process was slow and
communication inadequate. Tok Pisin doesn't work very well on
paper and neither they nor I know how to write in Bahinemo. Letters
took months to return or were stolen or lost.

My article was warmly received, along with the pictures from Jay and Max. It was published in *National Geographic Magazine* in February of 1994.

I heard that at the end of their research, the scientists estimated that more than 40% of the plants on Mount Hunstein are found only on its slopes.

A couple of years ago, my brother, Tom, ran across a "Green Light Trust" organization from England who were taking an interest in the situation. When I called them, they told me they went to Wagu and took Moyali's son, Mathew, back to England with them, along with someone named Lukas. They sent me a book they had written called *Trees of Paradise* (Authors Richard Edmunds and Nigel Hughes, Green Press, 1991) in which they chronicled their own trip over the Hunstein Range to the distant Bahinemo village of Gahom. For all that, I was grateful, but what did it mean for Wagu and the trees?

Now, news comes suddenly in the form of seventeen pages of letters about the Bahinemos from my parents. They have travelled to Wagu on a U.S. government grant to document the endangered Bahinemo language before it becomes extinct. There is so much news that I find it overwhelming. What follows is a distillation of their letters:

Once again, the generation I knew is no longer in charge and a new one has grown older. Ma Wamseli and San Moyali, from our trip up Mount Hunstein, have passed on, along with Ma Lekim.

Wamseli's widow, Yamu, the oldest on our trip, who made the seed soup and sago for us, outlived four husbands and is still strong. One of Wamseli's sons is the leader of a thriving church. Wamseli left behind several other children and many grandchildren. One granddaughter is named after me. Another person in the village named two of her children Gabriel and Sarah after my own. Clement, the eleven year old boy who went on the expedition with us, is married and a father, but is as shy as ever.

Ma Gogomo, the dynamic pastor who was first up Mount Hunstein, is healthy despite his age. He is still active in church and presides over a large family.

Ma Jim and San Bahio, our babysitters and best friends, have two boys who are now teenagers. Jim and Bahio have been extremely helpful to my parents. Ma Jim represents Wagu as the local government councilor.

Mathew, Moyali's son, has taken Moyali's place as the heir of the entire Wagu watershed and the land we explored. Apparently, he did go to both England and Australia, thanks to Green Light Trust. They helped him to see the importance of saving rainforests. He acted in a play on the coast championing saving trees. Now he is heavily involved in tourism in Wagu.

The self-serving doctor who was manipulating the village to his own ends has long disappeared and no one is sure where he went.

Andrew, who dreamed of starting a tourist business, went back to being a doctor. He is doing an excellent job, saving many lives and mending broken bones.

World Wildlife Fund put in a new clean water reservoir that serves the lower half of the village. The water supply has been a huge success.

Many old ways are gone. Bahinemo culture has definitely compromised with civilization. The old social system is showing strain. However, with the change has come an overall sense of well-being.

Life is easier for the women. There are no more unwieldy bark bowls. Cooking pots are much easier to use and last longer. The women have also switched completely from grass skirts to modern clothing which is easier to keep clean. They make their own. Most of all, sago trees, planted years ago right near the village are now ripe and ready for harvest, so there are fewer trips deep into the terrible, muddy sago swamp.

The men, for their part, are using nets entirely instead of spearing fish. Thus they have plenty of food for their families and do not have to hunt often. They build new stronger houses which last longer, though they still use forest materials. These changes free up a lot of time for the men.

There are no community sing-sings though the villagers still find joy in dancing a more modern style of dance. There is no men's cult. Not everyone goes to church, or even the same church, as there are two. There are no longer initiations, which were quite cruel. Polygamy and war don't exist, so there are now enough women to match up with the men. Young people who have gone to school believe they know much more than the few older people, and hence are running the village.

The last bastion of traditional Bahinemo life is a village called Namu. A few people still live there, deep in the rainforest, in order to hang on to their ancient ways. Namu is so far into the mountains that no one can get there without hiking. Apparently, there are only around 30 people in Namu.

I find it strange to hear there is a beach which goes all around the lake. Just as an introduced water weed destroyed the lake years ago, the government recently introduced Pacu fish from South America. They have multiplied like wild fire and eaten almost all of the vast march grass that once covered shores, shallows and floating islands. Shores are now barren and channels are hard to find in the vastness of the new lake width. Although there is less malaria, there are far fewer birds, crocodiles and native fish. The lilies are gone forever. I can't help wondering what else the Pacu has done to the ecosystem.

However, a most wonderful thing has happened. The villagers have found a tree in the forest at the end of the lake where birds of paradise gather every day to display their feathers and dance. Scientists call this a lekking tree. At least three to five males show off each morning. The magnificent birds are the traditional Lesser Birds of Paradise that are on the national flag. This sight is so rare that I can't imagine it is a coincidence that it is found so near the village. Normally, the birds would only be found several days walk into the rainforest where we heard the birds of paradise on our expedition. I think God himself sent them.

Several tourists come out each week and spend the night in order to view this wonderful sight early in the morning. A man named Alouis Mateos is responsible for this. He owns a lodge at Ambunti and has taken an interest in bringing tourists out to Wagu. He has guides who bring them in and cook their meals. Wagu villagers take them into the rainforest to see the birds.

In order to house these and other eco-tourists, Mathew built a very large guest house with four bedrooms and a huge living area. It has running water, a shower and a flush toilet. The front is eleven feet off of the ground with a magnificent view of the lake. This guest house is located between the village and the waterfall where Andrew and I dreamed of building one long ago.

Tourists bring a small but steady income to the village by paying for a guide, renting the house, and buying whatever souvenirs they find, including an occasional orchid or other tropical plant. Some also take the boat tour up the mouth of the Hunstein River into flood-plain forest as we did. Unfortunately, most of this wealth is not evenly shared by the villagers. Almost all of it goes to Mathew.

Mathew, his sister Wama and their friends are intermarrying with outsiders and inviting them into their clan. They are even alienating the true Bahinemos and accusing them of usurping Yalfei's land, the Tuhiyu clan of the eagle. The land that is the watershed for Wagu may primarily go to outsiders after all.

Tourism in Wagu is not the abusive old colonial style tourism we feared. In general, tourists are not tempted to gawk at the villagers' ceremonies and artifacts such as grass skirts since these no longer exist. In fact, because this new generation refuses to be seen topless, the village won't even put on a sing-sing as some tourist agencies demand. The beautiful two part harmony and the fervor of the dance with elaborate decorations are gone. There is one man who still makes carvings, but most of the villagers have stopped doing so because of their association with evil spirits.

Now, tourists come to Wagu to see the lake, the wildlife and the forest. Culture tourism is out. Eco-tourism is in. There are butterflies to collect and other birds and animals to see as well as the Birds of Paradise. Three cassowaries roam the village, for instance.

Trekking is starting to become popular. The Bahinemos have improved the trail to Bani so it doesn't go through the fetid sago swamp anymore. There are other potential camping spots such as Gipa, with its beautiful pools, waterfalls and cool air. One can get close to the wildlife there, and it is only a two day hike. Alouis already advertises an adventure trek to Gahom on the other side of

Mount Hunstein. Why not take our trail and climb Mount Hunstein itself? Or would that mar its beauty too much? There are still so many possibilities and unanswered questions.

There are only a few money making projects in the village besides ecotourism. Crocodile farming and dressmaking are examples. Andrew dreams of making money from oil palms.

Most other business ventures have failed. The politics of small enterprises and their competition with larger places in the world are too complex. My brother, Jamey, is collecting money to enlarge and advance the village school so future generations will be better equipped to make such endeavors succeed.

The whole village is now convinced that logging the area is a very bad idea. Mathew insists that the rainforest and the rivers, including Mount Hunstein, must remain in good shape.

At the very end of the letters from my parents I find the best news of all. Between the World Wildlife Fund, the East Sepik Council of Women, the Wagu villagers and an environmental organization in Ambunti, the Hunstein Rainforest has at last been made into a nature preserve!

Yes! The rainforest has been saved!

The *National Geographic* article and my time spent with the Bahinemos succeeded in drawing enough attention to the situation to defeat the multinational logging companies. My rendezvous with the rainforest was worth everything. If my nightmares of the bull-dozers were prophetic, we thwarted them.

Now if you look at a Google map of Papua New Guinea you will see the preserve prominently displayed. It is called "April Salome Forest Management Area."

How can one put a price on a rainforest? Some people who heard I was writing this book have asked me, "What value is there in a bunch of trees? Why not mine them for gold, oil and logs?" I hope those of you who have read this book will not need an answer to that question. You will already have one in your hearts. This was my rendezvous with a rainforest. I hope it is also yours and that you will have fallen in love with rainforests from the bottom part of your soul.

Someday future generations will go to Gipa and listen to the wind in the kauri pines, the waterfalls, the multitudes of birds and the drone of the cicadas. My grandchildren will be able to see a blue mountain swallow tail butterfly floating high above, and stand in the cool clear water below. They may taste tart waxy fruits and press their hands into the prints of a giant cassowary. Perhaps you too will get to curl up in a sleeping bag and listen to the thunder of a tropical storm and the crystal sounds of bats.

And I think at least through writing this book that I myself have been able to take these things inside, where they will be preserved forever.

The kitchen
of Mathew's
guest house

Moyali's daughter,
Wama, the new
tourist guide

Bird of paradise dancing

The Hunstein Range Wildlife Management Area

R A I N F O R E S T

Rivulets of crystal water
gush down the sides of my tarpaulin and
splash into pools of decayed leaves,
between roots of trees
in the emerald twilight of a rainforest.
All around me,
in lower places,
clear liquid cascades across mud,
sucks around small leafy plants
and leaps
into self made gullies.
In my sleeping bag,
under the frail plastic sheet,
I imagine myself a shrouded caterpillar
trying to adapt to a
more powerful world
than I once thought existed.
Never have I felt so vulnerable,
so tiny.
Forces beyond,
playfully display their power
in the sonic boom of thunder,
the random crash
of weak branches from above,
and the steady pelting of ripe fruit.

Old waterways begin,
first to trickle,
then to rush,
and finally
to roar
across the forest floor around me,
and I wonder
about the location and altitude
of my platform.
Rivers, in a healthy rainforest,
seldom rise above well worn flood zones,
I am told.
Easy to say,
but what if
my make-shift platform
stands in such a zone?
Slowly
the cacophony of sound
becomes a steady hypnotizing roar
and in helplessness,
I succumb
to the imaginary safety of
my nylon cocoon
and sleep.
Tomorrow,
bright colored flowers
will dance
to the songs of birds,
on a leafy canopy
under a warm drying
sun.

As of the year this book was published, the Hunstein Rainforest is still carefully guarded by the Bahinemo people and remains intact. They continue to search for ways to maintain financial stability.

Wagu Village Website: www.wagurainforest.com

edierainforest@yahoo.com

Further reading:
"Bakker, Edie, "Return to Hunstein Forest, *National Geographic* 185:2 (February 1994) pp. 40-63
Dye, T. Wayne and Sally Folger Dye, "A tale of three languages: language shift in a micro-context," *International Journal of Society and Language* 214 (2012): pp. 27-38

Appendix:

THE MEMBERS OF THE EXPEDITION
In alphabetical order:

Bahio [BAH-hee-oh] - Young wife of Jim from a neighboring rainforest tribe. Close friend and baby-sitter for the children of Rob and Edie during previous expedition.

Clement - nine-year old son of Bahinemos, Wamseli and Yamu.

Edie - American leader of the expedition and author of this book; raised in Papua New Guinea as the daughter of anthropologist/missionaries and adopted by the Bahinemos.

Gogomo - [KO-komo] - Hard working, smiling, enthusiastic Bahinemo pastor; always saving the day.

Jim - Young husband of Bahio; guide and close friend of Rob and Edie from previous expedition. Knows a little about Westerners and comprehends English.

Karl - Papua New Guinean botanist from the highlands but living in a modern home in Lae. Karl's job was to identify the plants Max photographed.

Lekim - [LAY-kim] - Elderly adopted Bahinemo "uncle" of author. Knows the "secrets of the forest" and the stories of the ancestors.

Mathew - teen-aged son of Moyali, heir to the land.

Max - Middle-aged professional photographer from New York, accustomed to photographing luxury tours around the world. The purpose of the whole trip was to enable Max to take rainforest photos.

Moyali [mo-YAH-ly] - red-headed widow and friend of Edie's mom. Moyali owns all of the land the expedition covered. Mother of Mathew.

Rob - Edie's Dutch husband, who had been in Papua New Guinea before; chaperone, handy-man and all-around support.

Wamseli [wahm-sully] - Father of Clement and husband of Yamu.

Bahinemo man who worked for Edie's parents as a boy.

Yamu - [YAH-moo] - Strong, quiet, mature Bahinemo wife of Wamseli

230